LIGHT and OPTICS

PHYSICS IN
OUR WORLD

LIGHT and OPTICS

Kyle Kirkland, Ph.D.

Facts On File

An imprint of Infobase Publishing

LIGHT AND OPTICS

Facts On File, Inc.
An imprint of Infobase Publishing
132 West 31st Street
New York NY 10001

ISBN-10: 0-8160-6114-9
ISBN-13: 978-0-8160-6114-3

Library of Congress Cataloging-in-Publication Data

Kirkland, Kyle.
    Light and optics / Kyle Kirkland.
        p. cm.—(Physics in our world)
    Includes bibliographical references and index.
    ISBN 0-8160-6114-9 (acid-free paper)
    1. Light—Study and teaching (Secondary) 2. Electromagnetic waves—Study and Teaching (Secondary) 3. Optics—Study and Teaching (Secondary) I. Title.
    QC363.K576 2007
    535—dc22   2006018309

Facts On File books are available at special discounts when purchased in bulk quantities for businesses, associations, institutions, or sales promotions. Please call our Special Sales Department in New York at (212) 967-8800 or (800) 322-8755.

You can find Facts On File on the World Wide Web at http://www.factsonfile.com

Text design by Kerry Casey
Cover design by Dorothy M. Preston
Illustrations by Richard Garratt

Printed in the United States of America

MP FOF 10 9 8 7 6 5 4 3 2 1

This book is printed on acid-free paper.

This book is dedicated to Sara.
The light in me salutes the much
brighter light in you. Namaste.

✱ CONTENTS ✱

✳ PREFACE ✳

THE NUCLEAR BOMBS that ended World War II in 1945 were a convincing and frightening demonstration of the power of physics. A product of some of the best scientific minds in the world, the nuclear explosions devastated the Japanese cities of Hiroshima and Nagasaki, forcing Japan into an unconditional surrender. But even though the atomic bomb was the most dramatic example, physics and physicists made their presence felt throughout World War II. From dam-breaking bombs that skipped along the water to submerged mines that exploded when they magnetically sensed the presence of a ship's hull, the war was as much a scientific struggle as anything else.

World War II convinced everyone, including skeptical military leaders, that physics is an essential science. Yet the reach of this subject extends far beyond military applications. The principles of physics affect every part of the world and touch on all aspects of people's lives. Hurricanes, lightning, automobile engines, eyeglasses, skyscrapers, footballs, and even the way people walk and run must follow the dictates of scientific laws.

The relevance of physics in everyday life has often been overshadowed by topics such as nuclear weapons or the latest theories of how the universe began. Physics in Our World is a set of volumes that aims to explore the whole spectrum of applications, describing how physics influences technology and society, as well as helping people understand the nature and behavior of the universe and all its many interacting parts. The set covers the major branches of physics and includes the following titles:

- ♦ *Force and Motion*
- ♦ *Electricity and Magnetism*

♦ *Time and Thermodynamics*

♦ *Light and Optics*

♦ *Atoms and Materials*

♦ *Particles and the Universe*

Each volume explains the basic concepts of the subject and then discusses a variety of applications in which these concepts apply. Although physics is a mathematical subject, the focus of these books is on the ideas rather than the mathematics. Only simple equations are included. The reader does not need any special knowledge of mathematics, although an understanding of elementary algebra would be helpful in a few cases. The number of possible topics for each volume is practically limitless, but there is only room for a sample; regrettably, interesting applications had to be omitted. But each volume in the set explores a wide range of material, and all volumes contain a further reading and Web sites section that lists a selection of books and Web sites for continued exploration. This selection is also only a sample, offering suggestions of the many exploration opportunities available.

I was once at a conference in which a young student asked a group of professors whether he needed the latest edition of a physics textbook. One professor replied no, because the principles of physics "have not changed in years." This is true for the most part, but it is a testament to the power of physics. Another testament to physics is the astounding number of applications relying on these principles—and these applications continue to expand and change at an exceptionally rapid pace. Steam engines have yielded to the powerful internal combustion engines of race cars and fighter jets, and telephone wires are in the process of yielding to fiber optics, satellite communication, and cell phones. The goal of these books is to encourage the reader to see the relevance of physics in all directions and in every endeavor, at the present time as well as in the past and in the years to come.

✵ ACKNOWLEDGMENTS ✵

THANKS GO TO my teachers, many of whom did their best to put up with me and my undisciplined ways. Special thanks go to Drs. George Gerstein, Larry Palmer, and Stanley Schmidt for helping me find my way when I got lost. I also much appreciate the contributions of Jodie Rhodes, who helped launch this project; executive editor Frank K. Darmstadt and the editorial and production teams who pushed it along; and the many scientists, educators, and writers who provided some of their time and insight. Thanks most of all go to Elizabeth Kirkland, a super mom with extraordinary powers and a gift for using them wisely.

❊ INTRODUCTION ❊

SEVERAL THOUSAND YEARS ago people believed that vision involved the emission of some kind of radiation by the eye. Everyone realized the eyes are necessary—an eye injury causes a loss of vision—but people in ancient times imagined the eye sent out rays and bounced them off distant objects, providing a sense of vision by analyzing the returning radiation. If vision really worked this way, then eyesight would result from the eye actively exploring the environment.

But vision works differently. Arab scholar Abu Ali al-Hasan Ibn Al-Haitham (965–1040) correctly proposed that the eye receives radiation emitted by other sources; some of the radiation travels straight to the eye, which makes the source visible, and some of the radiation reaches the eye after bouncing off objects that do not otherwise emit radiation, which is how these objects become visible. The major source of this radiation, called light, is the Sun. Light is the messenger of vision, and the eye is tuned to detect it.

The importance of light in vision was an excellent motivator for scientists to study and experiment with this type of radiation, known as *electromagnetic radiation*. Optics is the study of light and the devices and instruments that make use of light. But visible light forms only a small portion of the broad range of radiation, and while the eye and instruments such as microscopes and telescopes are important topics, they do not by any means encompass the whole subject. *Light and Optics* adopts a physics perspective and explores the science of electromagnetic radiation and its tremendous variety of applications. The optics of image formation, described in chapter 2, is an essential aspect, but this volume also includes discussions of the intense beams of light produced by *lasers,* the role of light in biological processes such as photosynthesis and medical procedures such as laser surgery, astronomical observations based on all types of radiation, and applications involving communication, radar, and the transformation of light into electricity.

An understanding of the science of light led to ways of correcting faulty vision, as well as the means of improving vision to study objects too small or too distant to be seen by the unaided eye. The performance of instruments such as microscopes, telescopes, and the human eye depends on the principles of optics. But even with these advances, some mysteries remain. The nature of light has puzzled scientists for centuries, and just when people think they have it figured out, light does something different. Sometimes light behaves as fields of energy oscillating—vibrating—at various rates, and sometimes light behaves as if it consists of a stream of small particles. These two behaviors are entirely different, yet both are within light's amazing abilities. Whether future research will clear up this mystery or further deepen it is not presently known.

Devices such as cell phones and X-ray machines employ electromagnetic radiation that is different from visible light in the number of oscillations per second; X-ray machines use radiation having a much higher oscillation rate than light, and cell phones use radiation having a lower rate. Although all the types of electromagnetic radiation share many of the same properties, the subtle differences are critical and lead to widely varying applications. The various types of electromagnetic radiation are also crucial in understanding the universe, which contains radiation emitters of almost every conceivable variety.

Light has energy, and this energy is capable of extraordinary feats. The energy of sunlight is the basis of all life on Earth, for plants use it to make the food that feeds the world. When concentrated into a narrow laser beam, light can cut, burn, and even propel spaceships. People are just beginning to understand and appreciate the many things that the energy of light and other radiation can accomplish. Today's equipment and technology are already impressive, and the future holds even more promise.

Light and other types of radiation are even being used today in the same way people used to think vision worked. Although the eye does not emit visual rays—that idea was wrong—there is nothing to stop people from building devices that do, and from sending out these rays to extend their vision to observe distant airplanes and detect drivers who exceed posted speed limits. The science and technology of light, radiation, and optics are full of ideas, old and new, to help people see farther and better, and in many strange and unique ways.

1
LIGHT: ILLUMINATING THE UNIVERSE

The Milky Way galaxy contains 300 billion stars, but one star is more important to humans than all the rest. The Sun, an average star in the galaxy, shines brightly in Earth's sky because it is much

This cluster of stars, imaged by the *Hubble Space Telescope*, contains only a few of the billions of stars in the Milky Way galaxy. *(NASA/AURA/STScI)*

closer to Earth than the rest of the stars are. Earth revolves around the Sun at an average distance of 93,000,000 miles (149,000,000 km), whereas the next-closest star, Alpha Centauri, is 25 trillion miles (40 trillion km) away, 270,000 times farther than the Sun. (Alpha Centauri is actually three stars—a triple star system.) Light from the Sun is critical to all life on the planet.

This chapter describes the nature of light and concentrates on astronomical sources of light. The physics of light has a profound influence on almost all human activity, from biology to technology, and even though a small number of stars can be seen (under the best conditions only a few thousand stars can be seen with the unaided eye), astronomical light has shaped science and the way that people view themselves and the universe. The physics of light and astronomy have also revealed much about Earth—for example, the element helium exists on Earth but was first discovered in the Sun! Only after finding helium in the Sun did scientists look for and discover this element on the planet.

Light has always been as mysterious as it is important. Early cultures associated light with fire and considered the Sun and stars to be burning like a flame. Today scientists have a good understanding of what light seems to be. The word *seems* should be used here, because light remains mysterious—it can behave as a particle does, and it can behave as a wave does, even though particles and waves are different. But one thing scientists are sure about is that light is electromagnetic radiation.

Light and the Electromagnetic Spectrum

Electromagnetic radiation consists of changing *electric fields* and *magnetic fields* that travel through space. A field is a physicist's way of describing the effects of something. Electrical charges produce an electrical force that affects other electrical objects in the surrounding space, so physicists say that there is an electrical field in that space. The same holds for magnetism and magnetic fields. Fields exist in space and act on other objects. The important thing in terms of electromagnetic radiation is that changing electric and magnetic fields interact with one other, a process called electromagnetism. The electric and magnetic fields are constantly creating one another: An electric field that varies over time is a source of a magnetic field, and a magnetic field that varies over time is a source of an electric field. These fields propagate, one field producing the other and then the other producing it in turn. This is known as electromagnetic radiation, or *electromagnetic waves*.

Although light does not appear to be related to either electricity or magnetism, it is strongly related to both. In the 19th century, Scottish physicist James Clerk Maxwell (1831–79) discovered the basic equations describing electromagnetism, as discussed in chapter 7 of this book, and he proposed a theory that light is electromagnetic radiation. Maxwell's theory was supported a few years later by German physicist Heinrich Hertz (1857–94), who studied electromagnetic radiation in his laboratory. Light is one example of electromagnetic radiation.

One reason that light is so important is that it is necessary in order for people to see. The visual sense is the primary sense in humans, taking up a large portion of the brain's processing capacity. Most of the complex functions of the human brain are performed in the area known as the cerebral cortex—a set of cell layers on the surface of the brain—and half of the cerebral cortex in a human brain is in some manner involved in vision. Half is a large fraction, considering all the other functions of the brain.

Vision is possible only because the eyes are sensitive to light. Two thousand years ago people believed that the eye can see because it makes its own light, but this is not true. Eyes receive light, they do not generate it. Anything that produces light, such as the Sun or a lightbulb, is visible because of the light it makes, which the eyes receive. Anything that does not produce light, such as this book, is visible only because of the light that it reflects.

Because light travels so fast, people used to believe that light can travel from one place to another instantaneously—in other words, they believed that the *speed of light* was infinite. But light has a definite speed, and it is slower than "infinite." In a vacuum—empty space—light travels at 186,200 miles/second (300,000 km/s). (The speed of light in the air of Earth's atmosphere at sea level is slightly slower, roughly 186,100 miles/second. The speed is further reduced in denser materials.) This is amazingly fast, which explains why it seems to take no time for light to travel across a street or from one house to another. But it is not instantaneous. Light needs eight minutes to reach Earth from the Sun and 4.3 years to reach Earth from Alpha Centauri.

Electromagnetic radiation forms a *spectrum*—there are many different forms. As discussed in the sidebar below, the basis for telling the difference between these forms is the *frequency* of the radiation. Frequency is a measure of how often a periodic event changes over time. An oscillation, or wave, goes through a number of cycles per second, and the frequency of these cycles is

Frequency and Wavelength

Events that occur regularly, such as the swinging of a pendulum in a grandfather clock, go through the same cycle over and over again. For a pendulum, the cycle is a back-and-forth movement about the central point. For light and the rest of the electromagnetic spectrum, the cycles are variations in the electric and magnetic fields over time. Variations that occur over time can be drawn as a wave, as shown in the figure below, in which the magnitude is called the wave's *amplitude*. Electromagnetic radiation propagates in the form of time-varying electric and magnetic fields, and these fields are always oscillating. The frequency of this oscillation is given in cycles per second, which are called hertz after German physicist Heinrich Hertz.

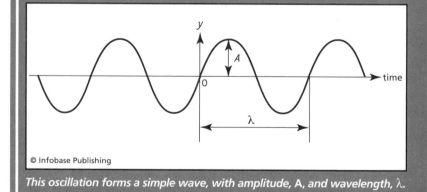

© Infobase Publishing

This oscillation forms a simple wave, with amplitude, A, and wavelength, λ.

called *hertz*. One hertz is one full cycle of the oscillation per second. Visible light is a type of electromagnetic radiation that has a high frequency, as its electric and magnetic fields are changing at a rate that ranges from about 425,000,000,000,000 to 750,000,000,000,000 hertz!

Other types of electromagnetic radiation include *radio waves, microwaves, infrared, ultraviolet, X-rays,* and *gamma rays.* The frequency ranges from the slowly oscillating 50,000-hertz radio waves to the high-frequency gamma rays of 3×10^{25} hertz or more (a frequency trillions of times greater than that of light). These types of radiation will be discussed in chapter 6.

In principle, one can measure frequency by using a stopwatch and counting the number of cycles passing by some fixed point in a given amount of time. But light, with a frequency of trillions of cycles per second, is too fast to be measured in this way. Scientists must use sensitive equipment that reveals the frequency of electromagnetic radiation. But there are also certain effects that depend on frequency and are so obvious that people do not need expensive equipment to distinguish them. One of the most obvious is the color of light. Color is strictly a perception of the brain—light, in and of itself, has no color, it simply consists of oscillating and propagating electric and magnetic fields. Color arises because of the way that the human eye and brain perceive light, and different frequencies evoke different colors—a person sees low-frequency light as red and high-frequency light as violet. The rest of the colors fall somewhere in between, as in the rainbow. Color will be discussed further in chapter 3.

Another important property of light is its *wavelength,* usually denoted λ. This distance is the length of one full cycle of the oscillation. An observer can determine the wavelength by measuring the speed, c, and frequency, f, of a wave; this is because the speed of the wave gives the distance the wave travels in a second, and the frequency gives the number of cycles per second. Dividing speed by frequency gives the length of one cycle, the wavelength:

$$\lambda = c/f.$$

Red light, for example, has a wavelength in a vacuum of 186,200 miles per second/430,000,000,000,000 hertz = 0.000027 inches (.0000675 cm or 675 nm).

Electromagnetic radiation consists of time-varying electric and magnetic fields traveling in space, but what gets these fields started in the first place? One way to do it is to accelerate an electrical charge. This is simply a property of electrical charges: When their speed changes, they emit radiation. The eerie lights sometimes seen in the sky at extreme northern and southern latitudes, for example, are emitted by charges traveling in space whose paths are affected by Earth's magnetic field. (In the North these lights are called aurora borealis; in the South, aurora australis.) Light is also emitted by atoms when their *electrons* (which have a negative charge) change position, and by bulbs emitting *incandescent light* as the electrons of the flowing current bump their way through the hot, thin filament.

The descriptions above, especially the terms *frequency* and *wavelength*, would certainly lead one to believe that light is a wave. The study of light has a long history, with times in which most physicists were convinced that light consists of particles and times in which most physicists were convinced that light consists of waves. Perhaps the strangest scientific fact about light is that today most physicists believe light is, or can be, both.

Waves and Particles

British physicist Sir Isaac Newton (1642–1727) believed that light consisted of high-speed particles traveling in straight lines. Although Dutch scientist Christiaan Huygens (1629–95) proposed that light is a wave, other physicists held Newton in such high regard that they accepted his theory with little question. But Thomas Young (1773–1829), a British physicist and physician, performed an experiment around 1800 that could be interpreted in no other way except to assume light is a wave. In the experiment, light from a small but bright source passed through two narrow rectangular slits onto a screen, as shown on page 7. If light was a stream of particles, the light hitting the screen would be two small rectangles of light. But what Young found was something entirely different—he saw a series of light and dark bands.

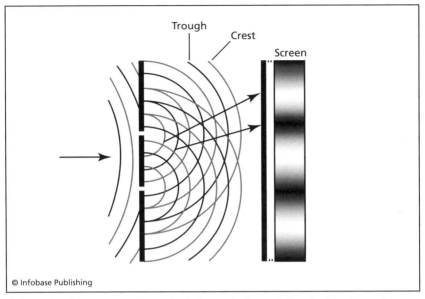

Trough | Crest | Screen

© Infobase Publishing

Light emitted by a source from the left travels through the double slits and onto the screen. The wave from each slit travels a slightly different route to the screen, which usually means that the two waves (one from each slit) travel slightly different distances to reach a given point on the screen. As a result, the waves may be at different parts of their cycle, one wave at a crest and one at a trough. The waves interfere (see figure on page 8), forming bright bands on the screen where crests align and dark bands where a crest and trough combine.

The bands formed because of a special property of waves. Imagine a wave as a series of crests and troughs as shown on page 8, like a wave on the ocean. When two or more waves overlap in space and in time, the waves combine. If the troughs and the crests of equally sized waves coincide, they combine to form a wave twice as big, as shown in the figure. But if the trough of one wave and the crest of another coincide, the sum is zero. The effect is similar to a positive number and a negative number of equal magnitude being added together. This process of combining waves is called *interference*. One wave interferes with another, and the result can be a bigger wave or a smaller wave, depending on how the crests and troughs line up.

Because light spreads out—this property of light is discussed below—the light from the two slits in Young's experiment

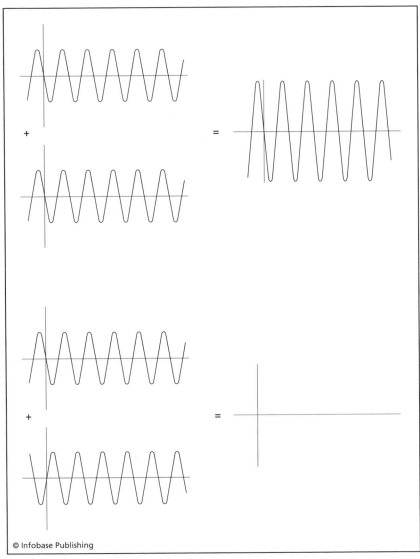

When waves occupy the same space they combine point by point. The two waves on top are in phase and combine to form a bigger wave. The two waves on the bottom are out of phase and produce a wave of zero amplitude—a flat line.

overlapped on the screen, resulting in interference. The bands of bright light were places where the crests added, and the dark bands were places where a crest and a trough cancelled each other. It seemed impossible to understand this experiment if light consisted of particles, because two particles of light would not add to zero.

Young's experiment was convincing. But then came other experiments and observations strongly suggesting that light consists of particles. When light is shined on a metal, for example, the energy of light will cause some of the electrons in the metal to fly off. This is called the photoelectric effect. If light were a wave, then one would expect the electrons to wait and absorb the energy as the crests and troughs of the wave repeatedly struck the metal. With a very weak source, an electron might wait a long time. This was not the case, however; electrons flew off right away and did not seem to be affected by the intensity of the light. German American physicist Albert Einstein (1879–1955) explained the photoelectric effect by proposing the existence of tiny particles of light called *photons*. When a photon of sufficient energy strikes an electron, the electron flies away at once. The theory fit well with several other observations and experiments and became widely accepted. (Although Einstein made many contributions to physics, the citation for his 1921 Nobel Prize in physics specifically mentioned his explanation of the photoelectric effect.)

So light was a wave—and a particle! What about Young's experiment? When the source of light in the double-slit experiment is exceptionally weak, emitting few photons, only one photon at a time passes through one slit or the other. If the screen is a light-sensitive detector, then it can produce a permanent recording of each photon as it strikes the screen, similar to a highly sensitive photographic film. After the experiment begins, a few spots of light appear on the screen, as expected by the passage of a few photons. But over time, the spots of light accumulate—and the interference pattern slowly emerges! It is as if the photons are interfering with themselves as they pass through the slits.

No one understands why this happens. Light has both wave and particle properties, even though these objects—waves and particles—are different. Waves are oscillations that are spread out over time and space, and particles are small bits of matter or energy. Yet light is both, and the same is true for the rest of the electromagnetic spectrum. Some people refer to light as a *wavicle*: part wave, part particle. But the nature of a wavicle is unknown and not readily conceivable. Throughout this book light will be referred to as particles or waves, depending on the situation. Until someone comes up with a better explanation, one must accept this strange behavior. Some physicists suggest that this is the best that science can ever do, but only time will tell whether people will continue to regard light as waves and particles, or whether people will finally achieve a deeper, and perhaps more satisfying, understanding of the nature of light.

Solar Radiation

Although the exact nature of light is uncertain, the primary source of light on Earth is not uncertain at all: It is the Sun. Light (and other electromagnetic radiation) from the Sun is called solar radiation (the word *solar* refers to the Sun). The next-brightest object in the sky, the Moon, shines because of reflected sunlight.

Solar radiation is important for many reasons. Sunlight gives people enough light to see, but it does much more than that. The oscillating electric and magnetic fields of electromagnetic waves—or the photons, in terms of particles—are a form of energy. Solar radiation provides an essential source of energy, without which there could be no life on Earth. Anyone who walks out into sunlight from a dark, cool building can feel the warmth and energy of solar radiation. Without the Sun, Earth would be a cold, dark, lifeless place.

Even small variations in the amount of sunlight can have large effects on the world's weather. Volcanic eruptions emit tons of smoke and gas into the atmosphere, and the emissions of a major eruption can block or absorb a significant amount of sunlight, preventing it from reaching the surface of the planet. The result is a period of cooler temperatures—sometimes enough to affect world events. In 1811, for example, a large volcano erupted in the Azores, a group of islands in the Atlantic Ocean about 1,000 miles (1,600 km) from Portugal's coast, and the eruption contributed to a bitterly cold winter in Europe the following year. This happened to be the year that French dictator Napoléon Bonaparte chose to invade Russia. Napoléon's troops were unprepared for the extreme weather, and the French forces suffered a devastating defeat that led to Napoléon's downfall a few years later. If Napoléon had been a better physicist, the history of Europe may well have been much different.

The Sun emits a lot of light, but visible light is only a small part of the electromagnetic spectrum. The Sun emits radiation at many different frequencies, with a little more than half of it in the part of the spectrum called infrared. Infrared got its name from the fact that its frequency is slightly lower (infra) to that of the lowest frequency of visible light, which is red. Infrared is therefore below red. The Sun also produces a lot of radiation at frequencies slightly higher than that of visible light, in the part of the spectrum called ultraviolet. Ultraviolet gets its name from the fact that its frequency is slightly higher (ultra) than the highest frequency of visible light, which is violet.

Although people cannot see either infrared or ultraviolet radiation, these parts of the electromagnetic spectrum have important effects. Infrared is associated with heating. Ultraviolet radiation turns human skin darker—it is responsible for suntans, as well as for sunburns. Ultraviolet radiation can harm living things because it can damage DNA, so skin cells respond by releasing pigment (coloring) molecules that absorb ultraviolet. This is what turns skin dark.

Fortunately, most of the Sun's ultraviolet emission is blocked by the atmosphere, particularly by the ozone layer, which contains an abundance of ozone (O_3) molecules. If it were not, people would not be able to go out in sunlight at all. Because of this filtering by the Earth's atmosphere of ultraviolet light and other dangerous radiation, the maximum amount of radiation reaching the surface of the planet is in a small part of the spectrum known as visible light. It is no accident that human eyes are sensitive to the part of the spectrum that contains more of the Sun's light (on Earth's surface) than any other part. During the daytime, there is always enough light with which to see.

Light from the Stars

Stars are distant suns. The points of light in the sky on a dark, clear night possibly give life to distant and maybe quite different planetary systems. But how do scientists know that these points of light are like the Sun, only far away? No one has ever visited another star or even gotten close.

Stars are so distant that their light, despite its enormous speed, requires years to reach Earth. The closest stars are so far away that they are seen from Earth as merely a point of light. This is true even if the light is collected and magnified by a huge telescope. (Telescopes will be discussed in more detail in the next chapter.) Planets like Mars or Venus appear as stars in the sky, but when their light (which is reflected sunlight) is magnified, a disk appears—the outline of the planet, containing enough points of light to resolve features such as clouds on Venus or the polar caps of Mars. The Moon is so close that its disk is visible even to the unaided eye, as is the Sun (but looking directly at the Sun damages the eyes—it is too bright). Even with a telescope, an observer can see no surface features of stars, since a star's image is a single speck of light. This is the reason a star's brightness varies—it "twinkles"—because Earth's atmosphere distorts light and causes point sources of light to fade in and out. This distortion affects the way a star is seen because it is only a single point of light, but light from nearby planets is composed of many points and not all are affected in the same way, so a planet does not twinkle. If an observer who understands the physics of light sees a "star" that never twinkles, he or she knows it must be a planet.

Astronomers quickly realized that they were not going to learn much about stars unless they learned how to analyze a tiny point of light. This they did, although the means of learning how to analyze light from the stars came from an interesting place—atoms.

Atoms emit light when their electrons change orbits around the positively charged *nucleus*. (The atom can be thought of as one or more electrons flying around a nucleus, although real atoms are more complicated than this.) Some electron orbits have more energy than others, and atoms give off this energy in the form of electromagnetic radiation when an electron makes a transition to a low-energy orbit.

There is an important relation between the amount of energy in electromagnetic radiation and its frequency. The energy of light and other forms of electromagnetic radiation is proportional to the frequency; violet light has a higher frequency than red light, and so the same amount of violet light—say, a single photon—has more energy than red light. Red light, in turn, has more energy than infrared radiation. X-rays, with their tremendously high frequency, have much greater energy than radio waves. This is why people must limit their exposure to X-rays, while no one is bothered that the air on the surface of Earth is filled with radio waves.

The relation between frequency and energy makes sense in terms of mechanics. Suppose, for example, a person wanted to make a wave in the water or along a rope. Making a wave that does not vary much over time requires little effort—low-frequency waves are easy. Making a high-frequency wave means that the arm and hand move back and forth very fast, which quickly gets tiring because it requires so much energy. Higher frequency means higher energy.

Atoms not only emit energy in the form of electromagnetic radiation but also absorb it. Atoms generally maintain a low level of energy, so if they absorb a lot of energy they usually emit it a short period of time later. The energy they absorb can come from different sources, such as heat energy; when a substance is hot enough, it has enough energy to emit electromagnetic radiation with the frequency (that is, the energy) of light. (Cooler materials also emit electromagnetic radiation, but it is of a lower energy—mostly infrared—which cannot be seen by the unaided eye.) As the temperature of the material rises, the material emits radiation of increasing energy. This means that as the material gets hotter, it emits red light, then light of a slightly higher energy, on up to blue. When it gets really hot it emits light of all energies, and this light looks white. (Therefore the highest temperature is "white hot.")

Astronomers discovered that by analyzing the color of starlight, they could determine the temperature of the surface of the star that emitted the light. This works for the Sun also; the Sun's surface temperature is average for a star and is roughly 10,500°F (5,815°C), and its light is yellow. Blue stars have higher surface temperatures; red stars have lower ones. (The temperature of the interior of a star is much hotter but cannot be measured by this method, because it is the surface that emits the light astronomers can detect.)

Another important discovery came when scientists found that different chemical elements absorb and emit different and quite specific amounts of energy. These amounts of energy corresponded to specific orbits of the electrons, which are the same for all atoms of a given element but different for atoms of the other elements. In terms of electromagnetic radiation, this means that an atom of carbon absorbs and emits different energies—and therefore different frequencies—than, say, an atom of hydrogen.

This became a wonderful tool in the hands of astronomers and physicists. A little point of light from a distant star may not be much in magnitude, but hidden within that light is a record of how hot the surface is and what sort of elements are there. All that is required to read that record is to study the frequencies of the light, as described in the sidebar on page 15, "Absorption and Emission Spectrum."

When Joseph von Fraunhofer (1787–1826) began to study the spectrum of sunlight in the early 19th century, he discovered absorption lines. Although other people had seen these lines earlier, Fraunhofer was the first to analyze them carefully. He spread sunlight's spectrum into its component frequencies with a *prism*, which will be discussed in a later chapter, or other devices, such as gratings, which he perfected. Some of the frequencies were missing or much reduced, and Fraunhofer recorded the number and position of these absorption lines. Astronomers later realized that these frequencies were absorbed by the gaseous elements in the star—the absorption spectrum.

The absorption spectrum of a star or the Sun comes about because light is emitted from the dense core region and travels up to, and out of, the surface. Light emitted from solid or liquid materials, or from the dense interior of a star, is different from the emission spectrum of gas that is relatively sparse (such as the air in Earth's atmosphere). The atoms of solids and other dense mate-

Absorption and Emission Spectrum

The electrons in atoms can have only a specific set of energy levels. This is a principle of quantum mechanics, the theory that describes the properties and behavior of small particles like atoms. Suppose a container of a small amount of gas, consisting of hydrogen atoms, is heated. The heat supplies energy, and the electron in a hydrogen atom absorbs this energy—but only certain amounts, or packets, of energy are absorbed. Atoms then emit this energy as electromagnetic radiation (this is how an atom "cools off" when it absorbs energy). The energy of this radiation will have specific levels, which means that the frequency of the radiation can have only certain values, since the energy of electromagnetic radiation corresponds to frequency. The spectrum of this electromagnetic radiation therefore consists not of all possible frequencies in a given range but of a set of specific frequencies. This is the emission spectrum of the element hydrogen. Different elements and compounds have their own unique emission spectrum.

Now suppose someone shines a bright light through the gas. Assume that the bright light contains all the frequencies of visible light (it is "white" light, in other words). Because the atoms of the gas absorb certain frequencies, the amount of light at these frequencies will be reduced as the light travels through the gas. A person examining the spectrum of light passing through the gas will notice that some frequencies are missing or much reduced. This is the absorption spectrum of the gas, and it is the "negative," or opposite, of the emission spectrum. The emission spectrum consists of bright bands at the emitted frequencies; the absorption spectrum consists of dark bands at the absorbed frequencies, which are basically the same as the emitted frequencies.

In the experiment of shining a light through the gas, the atoms absorb light of certain frequencies and then eventually emit these frequencies as they "cool down." But the atoms emit this light in all directions, so the light of these frequencies is scattered over the whole room. A person studying the light after it has traveled through the gas will observe an absorption spectrum, and a person studying the light that is scattered across the room will observe an emission spectrum.

rials are so close together that they interact, and their emission spectrum tends to produce light of many different frequencies, which is known as a continuous spectrum. (Light coming from a hot stove element, for example, produces a continuous spectrum.) When such a light travels through the outer and less dense regions of the star, the result is similar to the experiment with light going through a small amount of gas, as described in the sidebar on page 15, "Absorption and Emission Spectrum."

There are thousands of absorption lines in the Sun's spectrum. By matching these lines with those found in laboratory experiments of various gases, astronomers could determine which elements were in the Sun. But there was one set of absorption lines that scientists had not seen on Earth. After further study, these lines turned out to be from a previously unknown element, which was named helium (from the Greek word *helios,* meaning *sun*). Helium does not react with many other elements, so chemists had not discovered its presence by chemical means. It was only after

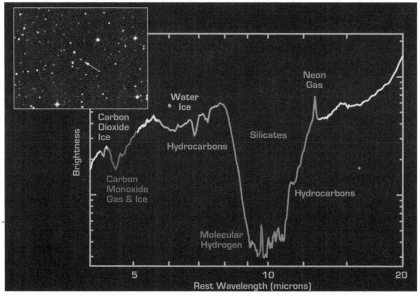

The spectrum shown here is from the distant galaxy indicated by the arrow (inset). This spectrum does not exhibit the narrow lines of absorption because the graph covers such a large range, but the varying brightness (vertical axis) of the wavelengths (frequencies) is due to absorption and emission by specific elements and compounds and reveals the presence of these substances. It is interesting to note that many of these substances are important for life. *(NASA-JPL)*

astronomers noticed this element in the Sun that it was searched for and found on Earth.

Scientists examined the spectrum of many stars and discovered that stars consist of elements similar to those that make up the Sun. Most stars, like the Sun, are gigantic balls of hydrogen gas, along with small amounts of other, heavier elements. The Sun proved to be a star, and stars proved to be distant suns.

Redshift and the Expanding Universe

Using powerful telescopes developed in the 18th and 19th centuries, astronomers discovered faint and fuzzy objects that they called nebulas. A few of these nebulas are vast clouds of dust and gas, visible only because they reflect the light from nearby stars. But astronomers eventually found that other nebulas shine because of their own light, and many of them are distant galaxies. Galaxies are huge collections of stars (and probably planets) like the Milky Way galaxy. Most of these galaxies are so far away that their light requires millions of years to make the journey to Earth.

People studied light from distant galaxies in the same way that Joseph von Fraunhofer studied light from the Sun and other stars. But when astronomers first began to study galaxies, they noticed that the spectrum of many of the galaxies had a curious feature. The absorption lines formed a recognizable pattern, but these lines were not in the same place in the spectrum as they were in the spectrum of nearby stars. The pattern was the same—the number of lines was roughly the same and the intervals between the lines were identical—and this suggested the presence of familiar elements. The problem was that all these lines had a lower frequency than in the spectrum of nearby stars. It was as if someone had taken the absorption or emission spectrum of a star and shifted it down, toward a lower frequency. The lowest frequency of visible light is red, and because the spectrum of distant galaxies was shifted toward the red, this phenomenon was called redshift.

What can cause a redshift? There are several possibilities, but one of the most familiar is known as the *Doppler effect,* as discussed in the sidebar on page 18. The Doppler effect arises when there

The Doppler Effect

Most people are familiar with the Doppler effect for sound waves. The horn of an approaching car or the whistle of an approaching train first rises in pitch—the frequency increases—and then, as the car or train passes and moves away, the pitch falls. The same thing happens when the wave is an electromagnetic one, such as light.

The Doppler effect is caused by motion. The source of the wave can be moving or the observer can be moving; it makes little difference as long as there is motion. Consider, for instance, what happens when the source of the wave is moving toward an observer. The source begins to emit a wave, and the wave begins its oscillation. But a wave requires some amount of time to complete. Before the wave can complete its oscillation, the source has moved. If the source is moving toward the observer, the source is closer to the observer when the wave finishes its oscillation than when the wave began its oscillation. This gives the emitted wave a shorter wavelength—and higher frequency—than it would have had if the source had not been moving, as shown in the figure on page 19. In other words, to the observer the wave is compressed and therefore seems to be of a higher frequency; this is called a *blueshift,* since blue is the highest frequency of visible light.

is relative motion between the source of a wave (such as a sound wave or an electromagnetic wave) and the observer (or listener) of the wave. When an object emitting a wave approaches the receiver, the frequency of the wave seems to increase (and its wavelength gets shorter). When the object moves away from the receiver, the frequency of the wave seems to decrease (and the wavelength gets longer). This is what appeared to be happening with the distant galaxies: They were moving away from Earth, so the electromagnetic waves they emitted were lower in frequency—shifted, in other words, toward the red end as measured by astronomers on Earth.

The Doppler effect might be able to explain the redshift, but it was puzzling that all the distant galaxies were moving away from

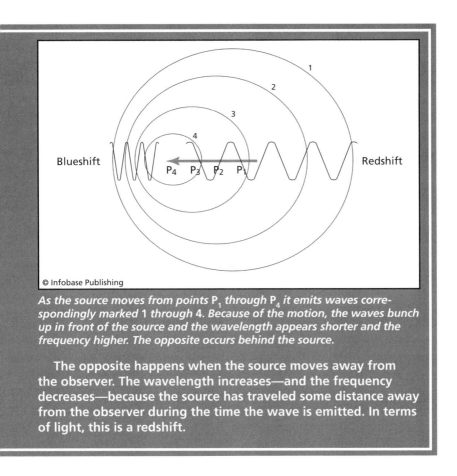

© Infobase Publishing

As the source moves from points P$_1$ through P$_4$ it emits waves correspondingly marked 1 through 4. Because of the motion, the waves bunch up in front of the source and the wavelength appears shorter and the frequency higher. The opposite occurs behind the source.

The opposite happens when the source moves away from the observer. The wavelength increases—and the frequency decreases—because the source has traveled some distance away from the observer during the time the wave is emitted. In terms of light, this is a redshift.

Earth. And the redshift was greater as the distance increased, so there was a pattern—this could not be by chance.

The redshift of distant galaxies, along with other observations and theoretical ideas, led to the development of the big bang theory. According to this theory, the universe began some 14 billion years ago when an immensely dense point of matter and energy exploded and expanded. The expansion continues, which is why the distant galaxies seem to be rushing headlong away from Earth. But the theory does not place Earth at the center of the universe—all distant objects in the universe are getting farther away from each other. Many scientists picture the universe as an expanding balloon, with the galaxies as dots on the balloon's surface. As the balloon expands the surface grows, and all the dots move away from each other, though none of them is at the center of the expansion. Some scientists consider the redshift to be due to the expansion of space itself, rather than to the motion of the galaxies, but the consequences for the spectrum of light are the same.

The study of light has revealed much, not only about light itself but also about the objects that emit light—the Sun, the stars, and galaxies. Even more than that, the study of light has brought about discoveries here on Earth, such as the element helium, and has provided hints as to the nature of the whole universe.

But the study of light is not yet complete. Light is still not perfectly understood, and although the topic has been hotly debated, most people continue to be puzzled by light's combination of wave and particle properties. Perhaps light is something entirely different, possibly different enough to be beyond the range of human comprehension. Scientists do not yet have all the answers. And so people continue to wonder about light, and about the many more secrets that the study of light might uncover.

2

OPTICS: IMAGING THE UNIVERSE

O N APRIL 25, 1990, the crew of the space shuttle *Discovery* placed the *Hubble Space Telescope* into orbit. The telescope became an important artificial satellite of Earth; roughly the size of a large truck, the *Hubble Space Telescope* allowed astronomers to view the universe from a point far above the distortions caused by Earth's atmosphere. Transmitters relayed the images to astronomers on the surface of the planet. Optics had moved into space in a big way.

Optics is the study of light and the devices, such as microscopes and telescopes, that focus light to form images. Of particular importance to astronomers is how light reflects from *mirrors* and how *lenses* bend and focus light. The bending of light is also responsible for some of the problems astronomers have with the atmosphere. These problems, and a few others, were solved by putting a telescope into space.

Bending and focusing light to make images is not easy. Optics can be difficult because light is hard to handle. Light's oscillations are extremely high in frequency—as discussed in the previous chapter, the frequency of visible light ranges from about 400 to 700 trillion hertz—and light is fast, traveling 186,200 miles/second (300,000 km/s) in a vacuum. Humans possess an excellent optical system—the eye and visual system—and yet the eyesight of many

The *Hubble Space Telescope* is seen here attached to the robotic arm of the space shuttle *Discovery* during a maintenance mission on February 19, 1997. *(NASA)*

people requires certain corrections. Even the *Hubble Space Telescope* was not flawless and required a significant correction, as astronomers discovered after the telescope was launched. The flaw was small, amounting to an error of about 0.00008 inches (0.0002 cm). This distance is only a small fraction of the diameter of a human hair, but sometimes in optics this is enough to cause a serious problem. Lenses and mirrors—and eyeballs—must be precise.

Lenses and Mirrors

Mirrors reflect most of the light that strikes them. The first mirrors used by humans were probably the smooth surfaces of ponds or lakes. Later, people learned that polished metals such as bronze also work.

Reflections from smooth surfaces like polished metal form an image, and people looking straight at a mirror can see themselves. But other smooth surfaces, such as a piece of paper, do not form an image. The reason for this has to do with the behavior of light rays. The previous chapter mentioned that light can sometimes appear to be a wave and sometimes a particle, but light can also be considered as rays that travel in straight lines and bounce off other objects.

A mirror works because the surface is so smooth that light rays bounce off in an orderly manner. If a jet of water hits a flat wall, for instance, a lot of the water bounces straight back; but if the jet of water hits a bush, the water flies off in all directions. The same goes for light. If a surface is smooth enough, most of the light rays are reflected back. But the surface has to be extremely smooth for this to happen, because light has such a tiny wavelength. Waves can get scattered by bumps that are about the same size as the wavelength. Since visible light has a wavelength of about 0.000016 to 0.000027 inches (400–700 nm), the bumps can be tiny and still scatter light, which is why a flat piece of paper is not an effective mirror. Although the paper feels smooth to a person's touch, to a ray of light the paper is mountainous!

Dressing room mirrors are usually flat and produce accurate images. Curved mirrors like those in a "fun house" distort images because the reflecting rays spread out. But other types of curved mirror are useful. In a *concave mirror,* shown in part (a) of the figure on page 24, the surface curves inward—the mirror is thin in the middle. If a concave mirror is in the shape of a paraboloid, then the light rays will converge to a point, as shown in the figure. (The geometric properties of a paraboloid are not the same as those of a sphere—a cross section of a paraboloid is generally a parabola, a curve such as the graph of the function x^2—but spherical shapes are often used instead of paraboloids because they are easier and cheaper to manufacture, although they cause a small amount of distortion in the image.) This is the way that many telescopes,

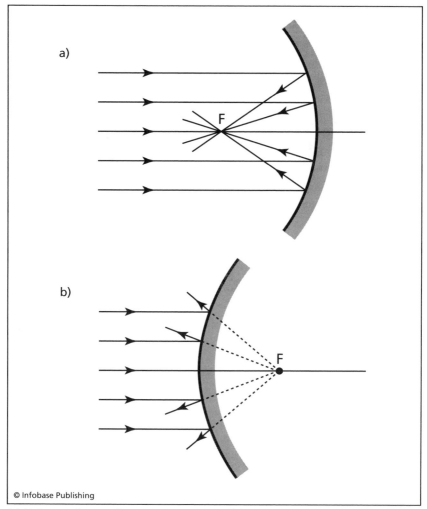

(a) Light rays from a distant source are parallel and strike the surface of this concave mirror. All of the reflected rays pass through a single point, *F,* the focal point. (b) In a convex mirror, the reflected rays diverge, appearing to come from a single point, *F.*

including the *Hubble Space Telescope,* gather and focus light. The point of convergence is called the *focal point.*

In a *convex mirror,* which is thicker in the middle, the reflected light rays spread out. As shown in part (b) of the figure, the rays from a convex mirror seem to come from a point, also called the focal point. There is some distortion, but convex mirrors give a wide field of view and are used in cars, at street corners, and in other locations where observers need to see objects such as oncoming cars over a broad area.

All objects that are visible reflect at least some of the light that hits them—otherwise they could not be seen, because people can only see things that either emit or reflect light. A few objects are *transparent*, allowing some of the light that hits them to pass through. Glass and water are two common examples. But something peculiar happens when light travels through materials like glass and water. Rays of light normally go straight, but when they pass from one substance to another they bend. Scientists use the term *refraction* to describe this phenomenon.

Ancient civilizations were certainly aware of refraction, although they could not explain it. For instance, people discovered that if a pebble was placed in the bottom of an empty metal cup, the pebble could not be seen unless the cup was viewed from directly above. But when the cup was full of water, the pebble could be seen from an angle. The reason for this is that light is bent at an angle as it

Convex mirrors provide a wide field of view, excellent for helping store managers keep an eye out for shoplifters and, as shown here, also effective in giving motorists a view of the road as they enter from a side street. *(Kyle Kirkland)*

comes out of the water, allowing the pebble to be seen even when viewed from the side. People also noticed that a stick submerged partway into a stream appeared to be bent at an angle, even though the stick was straight.

Refraction occurs because light slows down as it passes through matter. Imagine the light rays as columns of marching ants. When the columns enter a material at an angle, the first few columns of ants get bogged down, so they become slower. The rest of the columns keep going at full speed until they also reach the material.

Laws of Reflection and Refraction

The law of reflection is simple and was discovered a long time ago, certainly by the time of the ancient Greeks—Euclid described this law in his book on optics, written about 300 B.C.E., although no one knows the identity of the original discoverer.

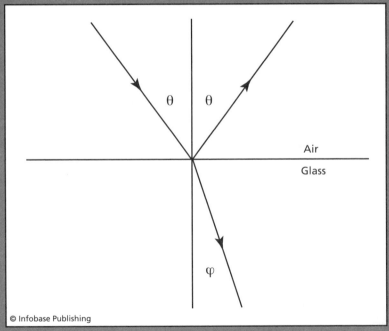

© Infobase Publishing

A light ray traveling through air meets the surface of a piece of glass at an angle of θ. Some rays are reflected through the same angle. Some rays pass through the glass but the angle is changed—the ray is bent.

Since the first columns of ants slowed down earlier, they fall behind. A line connecting the lead ants of each column will be skewed, or bent. This does not happen if the ants march into the material head-on or, in other words, perpendicularly (at a 90° angle)—then they all reach the material at the same time and the columns stay straight. The same is true for light rays: If light strikes the material perpendicularly, it is not bent. But when the rays strike at any other angle, refraction occurs. The laws of reflection and refraction are discussed in more detail in the sidebar on page 26.

As shown in the top portion of the figure, if a light ray traveling through air reflects from the surface of a piece of glass (or any material, such as a mirror), then it will take the indicated path. The line drawn through the center of the figure is the *normal axis*, which is perpendicular—it makes a 90° angle with the surface of the glass. (In optics, angles are usually measured with respect to the normal.) The law of reflection says that the angle θ (with respect to the normal) made by the reflected ray is the same as the original, or "incident", ray.

The law of refraction is more complicated. The law is easiest to understand when the angle made by the light rays is small. Suppose a ray of light travels through one material and into another. The materials can be air and glass, air and water, or any two different transparent substances. Assume that the light ray strikes the surface of a glass at a small angle θ and is transmitted instead of reflected, as shown in the bottom portion of the figure. The ray will be refracted and will make an angle φ with the normal, which is different than θ and approximately given by the formula:

$$\varphi = \frac{n_i}{n_r}$$

The numbers n_i and n_r depend on the materials and are called the *index of refraction* for that material (in the equation, n_r is the index of refraction for the material into which the ray travels, and n_i is for the material from which it came). The index of refraction for a material is a number greater than or equal to 1 and is related to how strongly light is bent when entering that material from a vacuum. Light is bent less when this number is close to 1.0; for example, air near sea level has an index of

(continued on next page)

(continued from previous page)
refraction equal to 1.0003, and when light enters air from a vacuum it is hardly bent at all. The index of refraction of water is about 1.33, and the index of refraction for diamond is 2.42. The equation says that φ is less than θ when light travels from a substance with a low index of refraction to one with a higher index, because in this case the fraction n_i divided by n_r is less than one. So if light travels from air to water, it is bent toward the normal. When light travels from air to diamond, it is bent a lot! When light travels from water to air, it bends in the opposite direction, away from the normal. (Note that people often measure angles in units called radians instead of in degrees, but that is not important in order to get an idea of what the equation is saying.)

This equation is an approximation of the law of refraction (also called Snell's law, in honor of its discoverer, Willebrord Snell [1591–1626], though no one knows for certain if Snell was the first to formulate it). The law of refraction is more accurately given by the equation $n_i \sin \theta = n_r \sin \varphi$, where *sin* is a trigonometric function. The approximation given above produces fairly accurate results for small angles because for such angles, $\sin \theta$ is roughly equal to θ.

Why do some light rays travel through a transparent object while other rays are reflected? A piece of glass, after all, reflects as well as transmits some of the light that strikes it. But physicists do not believe that the reflected light rays are any different than the transmitted rays. A set of equations and principles called quantum mechanics indicates that on a fundamental level, light rays and small objects behave in a statistical manner. Sometimes they do one thing, sometimes another. Overall, their behavior is consistent; for instance, a given piece of glass may reflect 20 percent of the light that hits it. But exactly which light rays are among the 20 percent is a matter of chance.

Lenses use refraction to bend and focus light. A lens is made of some transparent substance such as glass and is carefully shaped and polished. A *convex lens*, as shown on page 29, is thicker in the middle than at the edges. Light rays traveling through a lens are bent twice—coming in and going out. If the lens is shaped correctly then parallel rays will converge to a point, as seen in part (a)

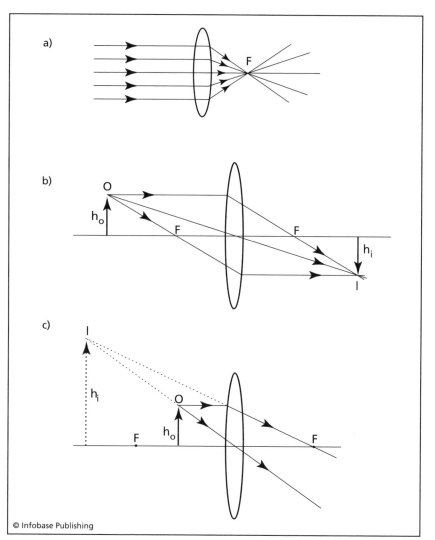

(a) Parallel rays converge to the focal point, F. (b) An object beyond the focal point makes an inverted image, h_i, that may be bigger or smaller than the object, h_o, depending on the lens and the exact distance. (c) An object closer than the focal point will be magnified but forms a virtual image.

of the figure. This point is called the focal point, similar to the focal point of the concave mirror described earlier. The focal length is the distance from the lens to the focal point. Focal lengths vary and are determined by the glass's index of refraction and the shape of the lens.

Light rays from an object move out in space in all directions. A convex lens uses its refractive power to bring those light rays together. If the object is at a distance greater than a convex lens's focal length, rays from each point of the object converge on the same location after traveling through the lens, as shown in part (b) of the figure. (If the object is remote, then the rays are essentially parallel, as shown in part [a] of the figure. From a great distance, the lens only "sees" a few rays that happen to be traveling on a nearly straight path to the lens; the other rays miss the lens entirely.) In the figure only a few rays from the top of the object are shown, but in reality each point of the object emits or reflects many rays. An image forms on the other side of the lens, although it is inverted (upside down). Precise converging is required to form a viewable image; otherwise, the image is blurry and indistinct.

Part (c) of the figure shows what happens when an object is closer to a convex lens than its focal length. In this case the rays spread out. However, a person looking through the lens will see an image, indicated by the inverted image (h_i) in the figure. The image is right side up in this case and is magnified. A convex lens acts as a magnifying lens for near objects, a fact well known to readers of the Sherlock Holmes detective stories.

How can an image form if the light rays do not converge? This is a special type of image called a *virtual image*. The lens spreads out the light rays in such a way that they appear to have come from h_p as shown in part (c) of the figure. A straight line drawn from each light ray emerging from the back of the lens will meet at the points indicated in the figure. It is as if the object were actually there, emitting (or reflecting) the light rays, instead of where it is really located. A person sees the virtual image because the eye focuses the light rays and forms an image that the brain assumes is the actual object. When Sherlock Holmes peers at a nearby object with his magnifier, his visual system focuses and interprets the light as if it had come from the "virtual" object. This is useful because the virtual object is enlarged.

The type of image shown in part (b) of the figure is called a *real image*. It is distinguished from a virtual image because it not only can be viewed by a person but also can form on a screen such as a blank wall, a piece of paper, or a photographic film. A virtual image cannot do this.

Human Vision

Images are essential for human vision and the eye is where the process begins. Light enters a person's eye through the pupil, which is the dark spot at the center. The pupil looks dark because it does its job quite well—it transmits most of the light and reflects little. In animals that are active at night, such as cats, the back of the eye contains a highly reflective substance called tapetum lucidum. This substance helps their eyes gather as much light as possible, although as a result some of the light is reflected back through the front of the eye. Because of this reflectivity, the eyes of these animals seem to shine at night when light hits them.

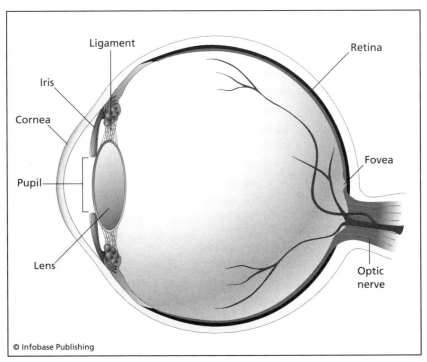

© Infobase Publishing

The human eye

When light rays travel through the air and into the eye they are refracted; the eye uses a lens to form an image—the same basic optics discussed in the previous section. A diagram of the human eye is shown on page 31.

The lens of the human eye is made of transparent layers, mostly water and molecules called proteins. But it is not the lens that does most of the work to form images; the cornea—the outer portion of the eye—does most of the refracting. The lens is for fine-tuning and can be shaped by small muscles, called ciliary muscles, to change the focus.

The shape of any lens influences which objects are focused in the image formed by the lens. When a person holds a finger about 12 inches (30 cm) in front of the eyes and focuses on it, the finger's image becomes sharp. But everything else becomes blurry; objects far behind the finger, as well as anything in front of the finger (for instance, the nose!), are not in focus. (The nose is too close ever to be in focus.) Lenses have a depth of field—this is the region in front of the lens in which objects will be focused. The same situation occurs with a camera lens, and, when taking a picture of an object, the photographer must get the object in focus. But adjustment of a camera's focus uses a different method than the one employed by the human eye: In a camera, focusing occurs when the lens moves in or out instead of changing shape. But objects beyond a certain range are far enough away that their light rays are parallel, and in this case the lens will focus all of them at its focal point. Camera users call this focusing at "infinity."

Since the cornea does most of the bending to make the images, people who have had their lenses removed can still see, although not as well and without the ability to make focal adjustments. Lens removal is necessary because when people age the lens sometimes becomes cloudy and blocks light, a condition called a cataract. But today there are artificial lenses that do a good job as replacements.

At the back of the eyeball is the *retina*. The retina contains more than 100 million tiny cells called *photoreceptors*. The image forms on the retina, and the photoreceptors transform light into the electrical signals that are the "language" of the brain. (The optics of a person's eye is frequently far from perfect, similar to the case of the *Hubble Space Telescope,* and the image is blurry. This situation will be discussed shortly.) The photoreceptors are 0.000079 to 0.0002 inches (0.0002 to 0.0005 cm) in diameter and contain molecules that change form as they absorb light. This change signals other molecules in the photoreceptor, which govern the flow of electrically charged particles called ions. The flow of ions transmits the information to other areas in the brain involved in vision.

There are certain situations in which all people have trouble seeing. For example, underwater vision is difficult because of the physics of refraction. The eye is accustomed to bending light a certain amount, based on the index of refraction of air—in which light usually travels—and the index of refraction of the cornea and lens. But the index of refraction of water is much greater than the index of refraction of air, and consequently the human eye's image-forming "equipment" is not as effective underwater.

This problem affects other animals as well. But a small fish called Cuatro Ojos that lives in South America and Central America developed a unique solution—it has four eyes! The fish swims near the surface, with part of its head raised above the water. One pair of eyes is above the waterline and works well with the refractive properties of air; the other pair of eyes is below and works well underwater. The fish gets a good view of both above and below.

Seeing 3-D: Stereoscopic Vision

Most people get along well with only two eyes. Even having two eyes might seem unnecessary—having only one eye, as was the case with a mythical creature called Cyclops, would appear to be good enough.

But there is a reason for having two eyes. The eyes are separated by a distance, and the average distance in humans is 2.5 inches (6.3 cm), though this varies among individuals. The distance is important because it gives the brain two separate and distinct pictures of the world. A person can see one of the two pictures distinctly by simply closing one eye; by rapidly alternating the closing of one eye and then the other, objects in the visual field seem to move slightly, because each eye sees them at a slightly different angle. The brain puts these two pictures together to make a single picture that contains information not only on the location of objects, but also on their depth. This is called stereoscopic vision, from the Greek words meaning solid (*stereos*) and watcher (*scopos*).

Flat pictures, whether they come from paintings, photographs, or television screens, can only give the viewer a sense of two-dimensional space: up and down, left and right. The real world is three-dimensional (3-D) because it includes depth. One eye can determine an object's location in two-dimensional space, but it cannot determine depth. A solid object may extend a good distance front and back, and it may be located closer or farther away from the viewer, but a single eye can only roughly estimate this distance because the eye can only generate a flat picture. But two eyes can do better, if each eye provides a different view. An object is in a slightly different location in the two views, as noted in the eye-closing experiment described above. The distance an object seems to move is related to its location in 3-D space. For instance, a finger held in front of the face seems to move a large distance in the eye-closing experiment, but a tree that is far away hardly moves at all. The brain measures the difference in the pictures provided by the two eyes and provides a sense of depth.

Astronomers do the same thing when they measure a star's *parallax*. Parallax refers to the apparent movement of an object when viewed from a different angle (as the objects appeared to move when viewed by each eye). To use this method, astronomers take pictures of the star at two different times. The pictures are different because Earth has moved during this interval. Astronomers then use the two pictures to measure parallax and determine the star's distance.

But there is a problem with this method: Stars are so far away that their apparent movement is extremely small. The apparent movement can be made larger by increasing the separation between the two views; if an object is viewed from two very different places, its apparent movement is much more noticeable. There is nothing people can do to increase the distance between their two eyes, but astronomers improve their view by taking the two

The white pole in the center foreground is in front of a distant tree (across the pond) and one side of a house. Compare the pole's position when the viewpoint shifts slightly, as shown below. *(Kyle Kirkland)*

This photograph shows the same scene as the figure above, but the camera is slightly to the left. The position of the white pole has moved with respect to the distant background. Note that the pole's orientation with respect to the nearby vertical twig on the left has not changed much. *(Kyle Kirkland)*

pictures six months apart. In six months' time, Earth has traveled one-half of its 12-month (yearly) orbit, and the distance between these two points is at a maximum—they are on opposite sides of an ellipse. The distance between these two "eyes" is enormous—roughly 186,000,000 miles (298,000,000 km)—so astronomers get a great stereoscopic view. Even with this technique, though, only the nearest stars show a measurable parallax.

Movies can be 3-D if two cameras are used, separated by a distance that is similar to the distance between the two human eyes. But the two films must be shown such that the left camera's film reaches only the left eye of the viewer, and the right camera's film reaches only the right eye. This can be done if each camera's film is slightly different from each other. (One way to do this is by *polarization,* which will be discussed later.) The films are shown on the screen at the same time, but the viewer uses a different lens over each eye so that only a single film's images enter each eye.

Correcting Faulty Vision

For the eye to function, an image must form on the retina. Light rays are bent by the cornea and the lens and, if all goes well, they meet on the retina. If all does not go well, objects are not in focus and blurred vision results.

A focused image requires proper refraction by the cornea and lens, and the retina must be located at the precise distance where the light rays converge. If the shape of the cornea and the lens is wrong, the light rays fail to converge on the retina. A lack of focus causes blurry vision called *astigmatism.* If the eyeball is the wrong size—too long or too short—then the retina will not be in the right place.

Myopia is the term used for nearsightedness. A nearsighted person can see close objects well but cannot focus on distant objects. The problem is that light rays tend to converge in front of the retina instead of directly on it, as indicated in part (b1) on page 37. The eyes can make adjustments to focus on nearby objects, but distant objects remain out of focus. In the United States, this common visual problem affects 25 to 35 percent of the population.

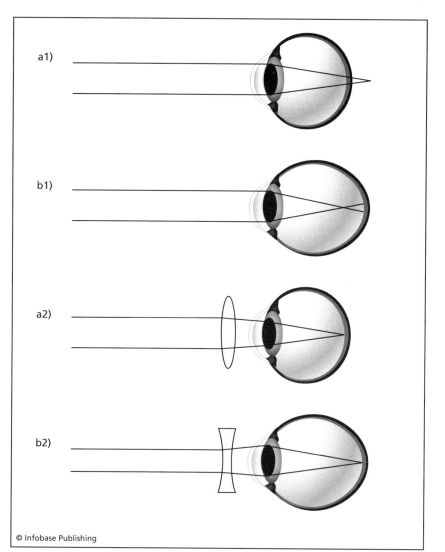

(a1) When the eyeball or the lens is not the right shape, images are not formed on the retina. In the case shown here, the eye is too short and the result is hyperopia, or farsightedness. (a2) A convex lens gives the light rays some extra convergence and the image forms on the retina. (b1) The image forms in front of the retina in an eyeball that is too long, resulting in myopia, or nearsightedness. (b2) A concave lens diverges the light rays so that when they pass through the lens, an image forms correctly on the retina.

To correct for nearsightedness, the light rays must be spread out a little bit before they enter the eye. This can be done by using a *concave lens* that causes light to spread, or diverge. As shown in part (b2) of the figure on page 37, a concave lens is thinner in the middle than at the edges. Light traveling through the lens spreads out because of the concave shape—the rays move outward. A lens of just the right shape will correct a nearsighted person's vision, because the additional spreading out moves the convergence point back a small distance and the eye focuses the image exactly on the retina. Each person's eyes are slightly different, so the correct shape of the lens will be a little different for each person. Lenses must be prescribed, or fitted to the person.

Eyeglasses used to be the only way to wear a lens. Eyeglasses are not a new idea; they have been around since at least the 13th century, and possibly earlier. But today there are other options. Contact lenses fit soft lenses on the eyeballs, so the user does not need to wear a frame to hold the lenses in place. Other corrective procedures include reshaping the eyeball with precise instruments called lasers. Lasers will be discussed in a later chapter.

Another visual problem is farsightedness or *hyperopia*. This is the opposite of nearsightedness: A farsighted person can see distant objects but has trouble focusing on nearby objects. Many people are slightly farsighted; the light rays meet at a point behind the retina instead of directly on it, as shown in part (a1) of the figure on page 37. In fact, everyone starts out that way—babies are farsighted. In most babies the eye grows such that in few years it can focus on nearby objects fairly well. But for some people the eye continues to be slightly off. The correction action is the opposite for that of nearsightedness—and uses the opposite type of lens. (See part [a2] of the figure.)

Considering the long period of time that people have been studying vision and making lenses, it is surprising that no one is sure exactly why visual problems develop. Scientists understand the optics of the eye, but they do not understand how the eye forms. Farsightedness is known to be a normal component of the aging process because the eye gradually loses its ability to focus on nearby objects. But no one is certain why a young person's eyes sometimes fail to develop properly. Myopia may occur because of an error in a person's genes, or the problem may be due at least in part to something a person does or experiences. Some people believe that focusing too often on nearby objects, such as books, computer screens, and televisions, can cause nearsightedness. According to this idea, the eye develops a tendency to focus on nearby objects, so that distant objects become blurry. But this is controversial, and many physicians do not think it is true. Scientists are doing research on these questions, and until firm answers emerge it is safe to say that the physics of the eye is much better understood than its physiology.

Mirages and Illusions

Faulty vision is not always due to the eye. This is the case with *mirages* and illusions—"tricks" played by nature.

Illusions are deceptions. One of the best-known illusions is the Müller-Lyer illusion. One version of this illusion presents two horizontal lines capped by arrows, as shown in the figure below. The arrows of one line point inward, and the arrows of the other line point outward. When asked which line is longer, most people choose the line with the arrows pointing inward (shown at bottom in the figure). This line may appear to be longer, but it is not. The

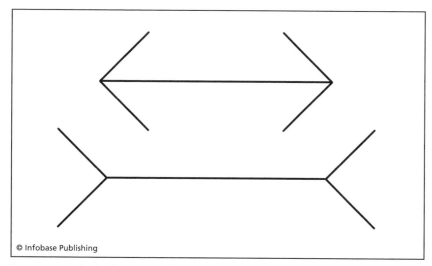

© Infobase Publishing

To most people the line on the bottom looks longer. A ruler says otherwise.

two lines are the same length. (Skeptics may wish to obtain a ruler and prove to themselves that this is true.)

The misinterpretation that occurs in the Müller-Lyer illusion lies in the brain and how it perceives optical phenomena. The brain creates the visual world that people see. The eye reports light and dark, lines and curves, and spots and dots. From these simple elements the brain constructs images and patterns. A visual scene is nothing but a bunch of lines and shadings, but the brain interprets them as cars, people, streets, and other objects. Consider that with just a few strokes of a pencil, artists can draw simple images, which people are able to recognize.

Most of the time the perceptions generated by the brain are accurate, but sometimes they are not. The brain can be fooled, as in the Müller-Lyer illusion. In this case the brain may be interpreting the inward-pointing arrows as an indication that this particular line is more distant. If this is true, then the line might be seen as bigger because the brain compensates for the extra distance. The brain often does this as a way of perceiving the actual size of an object, instead of the size of its image. For instance, a horse viewed at a distance looks very small, but the brain knows that it is actually a large mammal and so the horse is perceived as being bigger than its small, distant image would make it appear.

Mirages are also illusions, but they are not based on misperceptions. A mirage is an optical phenomenon; in a sense it is not real, but in another sense it is. A mirage is an image of an object or objects that are not where they should be. The object is real, but the mirage displays a false image of it. Cameras can photograph mirages, for the camera lens and film will "see" the same thing that the eye and brain do.

Refraction causes mirages. An earlier section of this chapter described refraction as the bending of light rays as they pass from one substance to another. Refraction (and reflection) can also occur when light rays travel through a single substance that has a varying density. The density of air, for example, varies both with altitude—higher altitudes contain much less air—and with temperature. Warm temperatures cause the air molecules to move around with greater speeds, which means that the air expands and therefore decreases in density. (This is the reason warm air rises.) Air at different densities refracts light rays for the same reason as discussed earlier: Light slows down slightly when it travels through air that has a higher density.

One of the most common mirages is the appearance of water as a person views a long stretch of road. The mirage usually occurs in the summer, on a sunny day, when the road surface becomes hot. The air just above the road gets heated, and light coming from above gets bent as it travels through this air. These light rays sometimes get bent so much that they miss the ground and proceed sideways or climb upward again. A viewer at a distance sees these light rays as coming from close to the ground, so the light appears to be from the surface. The image looks like a shimmering pool of water on the road, but the "water" is actually light from the sky.

If the atmosphere contains layers of different densities, these layers may cause the light to bend in such a way that it follows the curvature of Earth for a short distance. In such cases objects that are past the horizon may become visible. Some refraction always occurs in the atmosphere, so a little distortion is continually present. But in mirages, the image shows up in a peculiar place and often in a peculiar way, for the Earth's curvature can create an effect similar to that of a curved lens. The image may be magnified and inverted, and it can appear quite a distance above the horizon. The image may also jump or twinkle as the air in the atmosphere shifts and the densities and temperatures change.

Mirages may be responsible for a number of legends. The Flying Dutchman is a legendary ship captain who was punished for his sins by being forced to sail through stormy weather for eternity. Sailors rounding the Cape of Good Hope, at the southern tip of Africa, sometimes reported seeing a ghostly ship belonging to the Flying Dutchman. Perhaps what they were seeing was a mirage—a real ship, though a distant one whose image was distorted and magnified by refraction. The image may have been magnified, shimmering, sailing above the water, and possibly even sailing upside down—an excellent example of a ghostly ship!

Microscopes and Telescopes

Refracted light can do strange things, such as form mirages. But refracted light can be highly useful, especially to people in need of corrective vision. It can also help everyone see things that would otherwise be invisible.

Magnifying glasses have already been mentioned in a previous section. But even more powerful lenses can be used to create greater magnification. This is what a microscope does.

No one knows exactly how and when the first microscope was invented, although the basic idea seems to have come from Holland in the late 16th century. One of the most gifted of the early microscope makers was a Dutchman, Antoni van Leeuwenhoek (1632–1723). He made simple microscopes consisting of a single, well-crafted lens. These instruments allowed him to see whole new worlds of miniature life teeming in drops of water. He also examined scrapings from teeth under the microscope and discovered plenty of life there as well—which is the reason the wise people of today are careful to brush and floss their teeth.

Most of the powerful microscopes of today use two lenses. These compound microscopes have a lens called an objective lens to gather the light and another lens, the eyepiece, to magnify the image. The objective lens must gather light from a tiny area; usually it needs some help, and microscopes have a bright source of light to shine on the object being studied. Most microscopes have a changeable objective lens so that users can vary the instrument's properties. Lenses that are more round in shape, for example, let the user zoom in on smaller areas. The eyepiece is a magnifying lens, resembling the convex lens magnifier discussed earlier.

Although microscopes allow observation of tiny objects, microscopes that use light are necessarily limited by the properties of light. Objects that are not big and sturdy enough to reflect a significant amount of light cannot be seen. Atoms, for example, are too small to be seen by people, even using light microscopes.

(There are microscopes that "see" atoms but they do not use visible light.)

There is also another limitation of light microscopes. This limitation is due to the fact that light naturally bends or spreads out a little bit, especially when it encounters an obstruction. This phenomenon is called *diffraction*. As light travels through the small openings of a microscope it diffracts a small amount. The problem is that diffraction causes the light waves to interfere with one another, and the result is similar to that of the slit experiments described in the last chapter—light and dark bands form. Interference limits the *resolution* of the instrument because the light and dark bands will blur the smallest objects in the image. Resolution refers to the ability to distinguish small objects. Because of diffraction, light microscopes cannot obtain clear images from objects smaller than about 0.000008 inches (0.00002 cm).

The desire to see very small objects was the basis for microscopes. A similar instrument, the telescope, allows the user to see distant objects. When Italian physicist Galileo Galilei (1564–1642) heard about the new magnifying lenses being built in Holland and elsewhere, he decided to try them out for himself. Making his own telescope, he turned it to the sky and made many wonderful discoveries. Galileo saw the phases of Venus, the satellites of Jupiter, and hills and valleys on the Moon.

A refracting telescope resembles a microscope in its use of two lenses: an objective lens to gather the light and another lens, the eyepiece, to magnify the image. But the main goal of a telescope's objective lens is to gather as much light as possible, because the objects under study are usually extremely dim. The objective lens is therefore large, and telescopes are generally described by the diameter of this lens. A 4-inch (10-cm) refracting telescope, for instance, has a lens of 4 inches (10 cm) in diameter.

Refracting telescopes work well, but there are several problems. For one thing, lenses tend to focus different frequencies of light in slightly different places. This is a problem because the white light

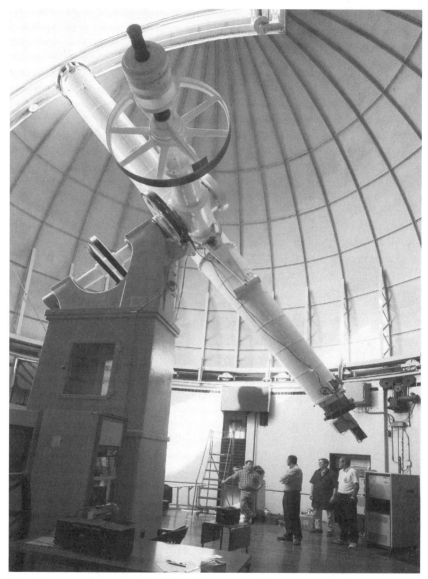

This telescope, located at the United States Naval Observatory in Washington, D.C., is a 26-inch (65-cm) refractor. *(United States Navy/Chief Warrant Officer 4 Seth Rossman)*

from an object will be separated into its component colors, each of which forms its own image in a slightly different place. The result is a blurry image. This effect is called *chromatic aberration.*

Another problem is that when lenses get too big, they sag in the middle. Optics requires extreme precision, and any sagging will ruin the lens. Refracting telescopes must, therefore, be limited in size.

Reflecting telescopes do not suffer from these problems. A reflecting telescope uses a mirror to gather the light. The mirror can be a concave mirror, as shown earlier, which reflects light onto a focal point. Mirrors have no chromatic aberration and they can be supported in the middle, so that they do not sag. All the largest telescopes in the world are reflecting telescopes. The Hale telescope at Palomar Observatory in California, for example, uses a mirror with a diameter of 200 inches (5 m). The *Hubble Space Telescope* uses a mirror with a diameter of 94.5 inches (2.4 m). There is always another set of mirrors or lenses in a reflecting telescope, to magnify the image and to reflect it from inside the telescope. The light converges in front of the mirror, but this is not where the astronomer wants the image to form—if it did then astronomers would block light when they poked their head in the telescope to see it! A small mirror reflects the converging light rays so that they can be focused and magnified off to the side.

Reflecting telescopes can be huge, but there is a limit here as well. Large mirrors are heavy, and even if they are supported they tend to lose their shape because of their weight. Today's biggest telescopes get around this difficulty by using more than one main mirror. If the mirrors are aligned properly they can work together and collect the same amount of light as a much larger single mirror can. The Keck telescope, at the observatory on Mauna Kea, in Hawaii, has 36 small mirrors that do the work of one 394-inch (10-m) mirror.

Perhaps the biggest problem with telescopes, though, affects any kind of telescope—at least the ones based on the surface of the planet. Mirages show the power of the atmosphere to bend and distort light. In astronomy distortion is particularly unfortunate, as it compromises the ability to study distant, faint objects. All the major optical telescopes are located on mountains in order to get

These observatories are located near the top of Haleakala ("House of the Sun"), a 10,023-foot (3,055-m) dormant volcano on the Hawaiian island of Maui. *(Kyle Kirkland)*

above as much of the atmosphere as possible. (Mountaintops are also dark—not much stray light coming from the cities—which also helps.)

Even better is to escape the atmosphere entirely; this was the motivation in launching the *Hubble Space Telescope*. This telescope orbits Earth at an altitude of 375 miles (600 km), well above the atmosphere, completing a revolution about once every hour and a half. Even with that great speed—roughly 17,000 miles per hour (27,200 km/h)—the telescope can stay locked onto astronomical targets for hours.

Astronomers were heartbroken when they found, soon after the telescope was launched in 1990, that its optics had a defect. The problem was a fault in the main mirror that kept it from focusing as well as it should. The fault, as mentioned earlier, was only about 0.00008 inches (0.0002 cm), but it was significant. Fortunately, scientists were able to develop a system of small mirrors that corrected the defect, and space shuttle astronauts installed these "eyeglasses" to fix the *Hubble Space Telescope* in 1993.

The *Hubble Space Telescope* has since delivered on its promise to reveal much about the universe. Astronomers have used the telescope to find strong evidence for a massive black hole in the center of the galaxy and to study the birth of new stars. Orbiting above the distorting air of the atmosphere, the *Hubble Space Telescope* has allowed astronomers to see much more detail than they ever would from Earth's surface.

Cameras and Photography

Lenses are needed to form images because otherwise light rays will not converge. If a piece of paper is held up to a window, no image will form because light from each point in the scene is scattered over the whole paper. There is no focus.

But suppose the light had to pass through a piece of cardboard with a tiny hole in it. With this cardboard in place over the window, the light would need to pass through the small hole—or aperture, as it is called—before reaching the paper. The light rays would not be scattered nearly as much, and an image of the scene outside the window would form on the paper. The image would be blurry because there would still be some scatter, depending on the size of the aperture.

The simple aperture is the basis for the earliest camera. A camera obscura, or pinhole camera, is a box with a small aperture on one side. (The term *camera obscura* refers to a dark [*obscura*] chamber [*camera*]). The aperture admits light into the box, and an image forms on the other side. The image is faint because only a small amount of light gets through the aperture, and unless the box is dark, the image will not be seen. Modern cameras are much more sophisticated, of course, but they get their name from this early device.

A pinhole camera can make an image only from an extremely bright source of light; otherwise, not enough light gets through the aperture. Letting more light into the box by making the aperture bigger was desirable, but early photographers avoided this because a bigger aperture meant a fuzzier image, due to increased scatter. But then in the middle of the 19th century, photographers realized that a lens placed in the aperture would focus the light. The lens formed an image even if the aperture was large, because the light rays were collected and focused instead of scattered. With a lens and a large aperture, cameras could form images even from relatively dark objects.

The first lenses were crude and produced poor images. More effective lenses had to be made from the most transparent material available, and they needed to be carefully shaped and polished. Today, lenses can produce crisp, clear images. But there is a range of lenses and cameras, and only the most expensive produce high-quality pictures for all kinds of lighting conditions and photographic subjects. Cheap lenses will do an adequate job but suffer from chromatic aberration and other imperfections, so the images are not as clear and sharp as they could be. As mentioned earlier, chromatic aberration causes a blurry image because the different frequencies of light are refracted differently and do not form an image at precisely the same spot. The best lenses are made from a variety of different glasses or plastics, each with a different index of refraction. The materials combine in such a way that the lens refracts each frequency of light identically—there is no chromatic aberration. Most microscope and telescope lenses are also made from a combination of materials.

Photographic film consists of chemicals that turn dark when exposed to light. This means that the film forms a negative: It is dark where the image is light and light where the image is dark, which is just the opposite, or negative, of the image. In order to make a print, film developers shine a light through the negative onto light-sensitive paper. This second process reproduces the original image. It is a negative of the first negative, and therefore it restores the light and dark parts to what they were in the original.

Many cameras today have replaced film with electronic light sensors. The lens forms an image as before, but the camera con-

The *Mars Reconnaissance Orbiter,* launched on August 12, 2005, has a camera called HiRISE (High Resolution Imaging Science Experiment) that can take pictures of objects as small as 3.3 feet (1 m) as the satellite orbits Mars from a height of about 100–200 miles (160–320 km). The camera in this illustration is located in the lower center, covered with a dark blanket. *(NASA-JPL)*

verts the image into a series of numbers, called a digital representation. These digital cameras store the image the way a computer stores data. The numbers can be turned back into a viewable image by devices that read and correctly interpret the numbers, such as image-processing programs running on a computer.

Capturing an image and putting it on paper or storing it in digital form is an effective way to preserve memories. Biologists and astronomers also do this to preserve their data. But the tools that many of these scientists use, such as microscopes and telescopes, form virtual images. A virtual image does not show up on a screen, so scientists cannot simply put film next to the eyepiece of their instruments and take a photograph. Lenses are necessary in order to turn the virtual image into a real one, similar to the way that the human eye does.

Optical instruments like the microscope and the *Hubble Space Telescope* have greatly expanded the range of human knowledge. The physics of light and optics presents new worlds that exist in tiny drops of water and in the vast distances of the sky. The ability to take pictures of these worlds brings the knowledge and beauty to everyone. People do not need to travel to a telescope on a remote mountaintop in order to see a breathtaking image of a distant galaxy. With the right lenses and optical equipment, the new worlds that optics has opened up are available to all.

3

COLORS

THE WORLD IS full of color. Human beings have long used color for many different purposes; for example, in ancient times people mixed various minerals such as red ochre with animal fat (or, lacking that, with saliva) and painted colorful pictures on cave walls. Today people wear dyed clothes and eat dyed foods, drive painted cars, pause to admire rainbows and beautiful sunsets, and live in houses decorated with bright ornaments and pictures, pastel prints, or attractive wallpaper.

Some animals can also see color, but many cannot. A bullfighter may wave a red cape at a bull to invite a charge, but the red color does not anger the bull—the color is mostly for the audience's benefit. Bulls generally have such poor eyesight that they fail to see anything that is not moving, so matadors wave the cape to attract the bull's attention. Although cats have excellent vision, they do not see colors well, either. But monkeys have good color vision, as do goldfish.

What is color, and how do people and certain animals see it? Color depends on two factors: the brain of the observer and the physics of light.

Color Vision

Although color appears in some way attached to an object, it is not. The red color of a fire truck seems to be a property of the

Flowers decorate this lawn in Cheltenham Township, Pennsylvania *(Kyle Kirkland)*

truck itself, but instead the color is a feature of the human visual system.

As mentioned in chapter 2, the human eye contains more than 100 million cells called photoreceptors in the retina that convert light into the electrical signals used by the brain to process information. The photoreceptors work by absorbing light. German biologist Franz Boll noticed this in 1876 when he observed that frog retinas lose their color when exposed to light. The energy in light caused molecules called opsins in the photoreceptors to alter their shape, and in the process the reddish purple retina became pale and colorless.

Humans have four different types of opsin molecule, as described below, and each photoreceptor has one and only one type. Biologists classify photoreceptors into two classes—rods and cones—based on their physical shape. These two classes have not only a different shape but also a different function and different opsins. Rods have one type of opsin, and cones have one of the three other opsins.

Rod photoreceptors provide night vision and peripheral vision. These sensitive photoreceptors outnumber cones by about 20 to one and dominate all areas of the retina except the center. The retina links rods into a network; cells in the network act together, amplifying weak signals. Any light absorbed by the rods is likely to register in the brain, which makes these photoreceptors good for seeing when there is little light, such as at night.

The retina's central area, called the fovea, is the place where visual acuity is at a maximum—a person can see more details of an object while looking straight at it, focusing the image on the fovea. Packed tightly with cones, the fovea has few rods; cones work individually to pick out the smallest features of the object or scene. Cones are also responsible for color vision, and this is why a person's color vision exists only near the center of vision. If a person stares straight ahead and tries to view a colored object off to one side, he or she can see the object but determining its color is difficult. Colors are vivid when the image is on the fovea, but the absence of rods makes the fovea perform poorly at night; a dim star is more easily visible when the viewer looks a little to one side of it instead of directly at it.

Cones do not work by "detecting" color. As described in the sidebar, what the cones do is detect the wavelength of light. The brain turns this information into color.

Wavelength and Color

When light passes through a transparent prism—a triangular piece of glass—it spreads out into different colors, like a rainbow. Before Sir Isaac Newton came along, scientists believed that the prism did something to light to give it color. The correct explanation required the genius of Newton—and knowledge of the property of refraction.

Newton showed that "white" light is in reality a combination of all the colors. Blocking all the colors except one, he showed that passing individual colors through a second prism did not result in any additional color separation: Yellow light passed through a prism and remained yellow. In another experiment, Newton positioned a second prism such that it collected and combined all the colors of the first prism, and the result was white light.

Prisms do not generate colors; they merely refract the light. As discussed in chapter 2, when light travels through a material it slows down, and light rays appear bent if they strike the material at an angle. The amount of refraction depends both on the nature of the material and on the wavelength of light. (Because of the relation between the wavelength and frequency of light, one can also say refraction depends on the frequency.) A prism spreads white light into its component wavelengths because the shorter wavelengths bend more than the longer ones.

But the human visual system does not discern wavelength as the length of one cycle of the wave. Humans see color. The three types of cones underlie color perception because the opsin in each type is best suited for a different range of wavelengths. As shown in the figure, there are red, green, and blue cones, named after the spectral region in which they operate. (Rods are also tuned but they work together to provide vision

The color a person sees depends on the wavelength of the light striking the eye. The wavelength may have been separated and isolated by a prism, or it could have been selectively reflected by an object. Green plants, for example, are green because they absorb most of the wavelengths of light except that which corresponds to green (roughly 0.000021 inches or

in dim conditions.) Cones report which wavelengths are present, and the human brain interprets different wavelengths as being different colors. Red, for instance, has the longest wavelength of the spectrum, and violet has the shortest.

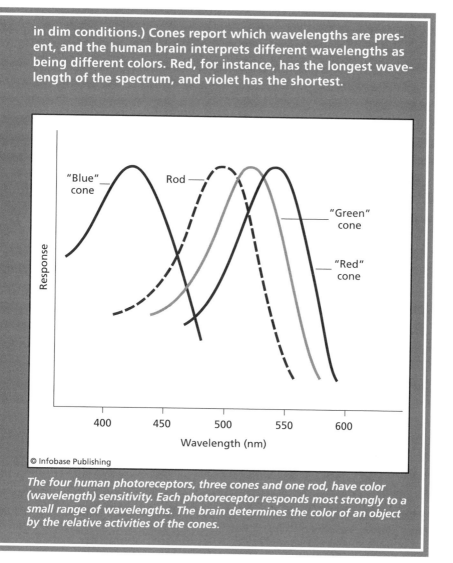

The four human photoreceptors, three cones and one rod, have color (wavelength) sensitivity. Each photoreceptor responds most strongly to a small range of wavelengths. The brain determines the color of an object by the relative activities of the cones.

530 nm). Specific wavelengths invoke specific colors. Mixtures of wavelengths also invoke colors (although people see the full range of wavelengths as "white"); millions of colors exist, distinguished easily—red versus green, for instance—or by subtle differences in shading, such as maroon and scarlet (two shades of red).

Not every person sees the entire range of color, because not everyone has all three cone opsins. Five to eight percent of males are color-blind, though in most cases the affected person can see at least some colors. (The condition affects many more males than females because it is associated with genes on the X chromosome, of which males have only one and females have two. Less than one percent of females are color-blind, since they are more likely to have at least one functional copy of the gene.) The most common type of color blindness arises from an inability to distinguish between red and green, both of which may look yellowish.

Color blindness is not a serious disability. Why, then, did color vision evolve? Why does the human visual system take the trouble to distinguish between different wavelengths of light? The answers to these questions are not fully known, but it is likely that color vision was important for activities such as food gathering. Seeds and ripe fruit that are good to eat can often be distinguished by the wavelength of light they reflect, in other words, by their color. Color vision enabled human ancestors to choose the tastiest treats and avoid those that were not quite ready or were poisonous. Today, shoppers at the market still choose lettuce, tangerines, and many other fruits and vegetables based at least partly on color.

Rainbows

Rainbows, like prisms, work by refraction, along with another optical property, reflection. Prisms use glass, whereas rainbows use water—tiny droplets of water suspended in the atmosphere.

Rainbows display arcs of color across the sky, separating white light into its spectrum. Rainbows are actually circular, though; observers usually see only part of the rainbow. Airplane passengers sometimes get a glimpse of the full, circular rainbow, because there is space both above and below their viewpoint.

Reflection and refraction of light by water drops creates the rainbow. Some light passes through the water, but a portion of it is reflected. If the drops are spherical—and most are—then the geometry is such that the reflection concentrates at an angle of about 42 degrees to the original beam of light. Some of this light will have been reflected after already passing through the rain-drop—reflection can occur at any surface, including the back side of a drop of water—and the passage through water refracts the light, separating the colors. The result is a rainbow; each wave-length comes from a slightly different angle, so to the observer the colors are spread out into bands.

Observers can see rainbows when the Sun is behind them and the sunlight makes an angle of about 42 degrees with their line of sight. The angle is important; otherwise, little of the light reflect-ing from the water droplets will be visible (noon, when the Sun is high in the sky, is not a good time for rainbow sightings). The best time for seeing a rainbow is after the passing of a morning or afternoon rain shower, when lots of water drops are in the vicin-ity. Rainbow hunters do not have to wait for stormy weather if they can find a water fountain that throws a lot of mist into the air; to see a rainbow, observers place themselves at the correct position with respect to a water fountain: facing the fountain, with the Sun behind them and at the proper angle.

Blue Skies, Red Sunsets

People observe a blue sky on Earth, thanks to a process known as *scattering*. Sunlight reaches the surface of Earth by a direct route and by more complicated, roundabout paths. The round-about paths are like zigzags, in which light bounces from point to point. The bouncing occurs because Earth's atmosphere consists of a huge number of air molecules, and many of these molecules interact with light. The molecules absorb light and then quickly reemit it, though not necessarily in the same direction that the light had been traveling. As a result, light scatters in all directions. A person standing on the surface of the planet sees a great ball of light in the sky, the Sun, as well as a smaller, less intense amount of light coming from everywhere else. (The Sun is bright enough to damage eyes and should never be viewed directly.) This scat-tered light forms the blue sky.

The reason the sky is blue is that air molecules are better at absorbing and reemitting the wavelengths of light corresponding to the color blue (the shorter wavelengths of the visible spectrum). Other wavelengths pass through with less interaction. Sunlight normally contains all the wavelengths of the spectrum, but the atmosphere scatters some of the blue and this is what people see when they gaze upward.

Sunsets and sunrises are reddish for the same reason. When the Sun is low in the sky, its light skims along the rim of the world, passing through a lot more atmosphere to get to the viewer than when it is overhead. This passage scatters out much of the blue, leaving the light colored yellow, orange, and red. Dust and other particles floating around the atmosphere can also scatter light at the shorter wavelengths, resulting in remarkably beautiful sunsets. In 1883 the island of Krakatau, located in Indonesia, exploded in a volcanic eruption that hurled a massive amount of ash and debris into the atmosphere. Sunsets in the Northern Hemisphere were particularly vivid for several years following this event.

Ocean sunsets, such as this one on the island of Oahu in Hawaii, are beautiful sights. *(Kyle Kirkland)*

Oil Slicks and Soap Bubbles

Another source of color comes from thin films—a coating of oil or the membrane of a soap bubble. These colors are due to a phenomenon of waves called interference.

Chapter 1 included a discussion of interference, the process by which two or more waves combine. (See figure on page 8.) Interference is important in thin films because light reflects from both sides of the film. The membrane, or film, of a soap bubble, for example, reflects about 5 percent of the light that hits it, and this is true of both the inner and outer surface of the membrane. The figure on page 60 illustrates this process. The two reflections reach the eye of the observer by traveling along different paths. The paths are not much different—the width of the film of a typical soap bubble may be only 1/250,000th of an inch (0.00001 cm)—but it is enough that the high-frequency electromagnetic waves composing light arrive out of phase (in other words, at different times during their cycle). Some of the waves destructively interfere—the crest and waves align, so the waves cancel—and some of the waves constructively interfere, building a bigger wave. Which of these occurs depends on the phase difference of the light from the two paths, and the phase depends on the wavelength. This is how colors arise: Light at one wavelength cancels (so that color disappears) but light at another adds together. The result is a spectrum, created not by refraction or scattering but because some of the wavelengths get canceled, leaving colored light instead of white light. (A similar process occurs when light reflects from the back of a CD or DVD.)

If an organism lacked the photoreceptors to distinguish wavelengths, it would still see the interference effects, but instead of colors it would see bright bands alternating with dark bands. The bright bands form where the light waves are in phase and the dark bands form where they are out of phase.

Although alternating light and dark bands are not particularly attractive, they can be useful: A careful measurement of these bands allows the thickness of a thin film to be determined. This technique is one form of *interferometry,* the use of wave interference to make measurements. To see the light and dark bands clearly, people often

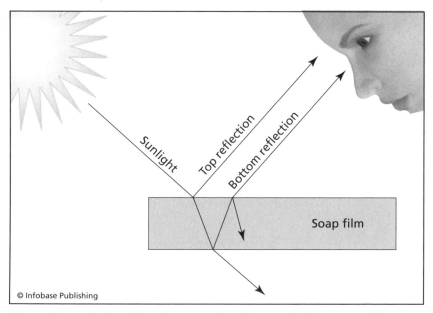

© Infobase Publishing

Most of the sunlight striking the outer edge of a soap bubble passes all the way through, but the film reflects a small amount. The transmitted light, refracted by the outer edge of the film, encounters the inner edge, which also reflects a fraction of the total. The reflections from the outer and inner edges travel different paths to the eye, and wave interference occurs.

perform interferometry with light of a single wavelength (color). *Monochromatic,* or single-colored, light does not spread into a spectrum and so the light adds or cancels to produce clearly defined bands. The sources of monochromatic light used most often today are lasers, the subject of the next chapter.

Interferometry can be used where other techniques of measuring thickness would be difficult or impossible. In 2003, Jason J. Nichols and P. Ewen King-Smith of the Ohio State University College of Optometry reported using interferometry to determine the thickness of tear films that coat contact lenses—the measurement being made while the lenses were in place on the eyes.

Color Printing

As mentioned earlier, objects that reflect light appear colored if they reflect only certain wavelengths and absorb the rest. A white object reflects all wavelengths equally well and a dark object absorbs most wavelengths, but an orange basketball absorbs all wavelengths except one (actually, a small number of wavelengths).

The United States Treasury Department introduced 20-dollar bills with some added color (besides green) in 2003, among other changes, in order to make a counterfeiter's job more difficult. Color printing is more difficult than monochromatic or black-and-white printing, as it usually involves a separate process for each color. But the basic principle is the same as with any colored object: The inks used in color printing contain substances that reflect a small range of light wavelengths and absorb the rest.

People can distinguish thousands of colors, and the best printers can reproduce many of them. Separately processing each of these colors would be far too expensive, so only a few inks are used—most of the time only four. Various combinations of these inks generate all the colors that make up the printed image. This process is similar to the method by which color televisions work; each dot on a television picture consists of three types of light—red, green, and blue—that combine to give the appropriate color of that spot. To portray a woman's red dress, the red light would be strongly lit and the green and blue off; a yellow jersey requires the red and green lights to switch on with about equal brightness, while the blue light remains off.

This process of color "mixing" is important because only a few colors, called *primary colors,* are necessary. But for printing and painting, the mixing is different than with television lights because inks subtract wavelengths, whereas television lights add them. The inks are colored because they absorb most wavelengths—they subtract these wavelengths from reflected light, in other words—and a mixture subtracts the wavelengths that each ink absorbs. Mixing inks gives a different result than mixing lights; red and green light combine to produce a yellow light, but red and green paint combine to produce a dark brown. For lights, the primary colors are usually red, green, and blue. For inks, the primary colors are cyan, magenta, and yellow. (Color printers add a fourth ink, black, because no combination of the colored inks gives a good, solid black.)

Despite all the colors that humans see, organisms lacking color vision might find the planet quite drab—a black-and-white world. This would be similar to what a person sees when a pure red light illuminates a green object. Under such conditions a green object looks black and is barely visible; the green object absorbs all wavelengths of light except green, and so it absorbs the red light and reflects little. But under the illumination of the Sun and other sources of "white" light, colors appear. The human visual system distinguishes wavelengths, which people perceive and enjoy as a rich and beautiful display of color.

4

LASERS

LIGHT PROVIDES THE basis for vision, optical instruments, and the beautiful colors that decorate the world. Light has gentle effects, conveying information in the form of visual signals and offering a soothing warmth that is absorbed by the skin of person on a sunny day.

But focused light can burn. Light emerging from a convex lens produces a tiny, concentrated spot of energy capable of igniting a fire. When a lens or some other object collects and concentrates enough light, the energy of electromagnetic radiation becomes more apparent. Light has long been used as a weapon in science fiction stories, with "death rays" zooming through space and incinerating the opponent's ships in battles illuminated by wildly swinging beams.

The emission of light by energetic particles is normally a random, *spontaneous* process; light spreads out, so its energy is not concentrated in small regions. Eyes or skin absorb such light without harm. Until the 1960s, as described below, weapons made of light were mostly fiction. Light could be focused but the necessary lenses and mirrors were too bulky and awkward to make effective beams. But then physicists discovered a process by which electromagnetic radiation is not spontaneous but controlled, and soon thereafter people were able to send beams of light racing through space.

Measuring the Distance to the Moon

Apollo 11 astronauts Neil Armstrong and Edwin "Buzz" Aldrin were the first people to land and walk on the Moon, in 1969. In addition to carrying out many experiments—and experiencing the exhilaration of stepping on the soil of another celestial body—these and other Apollo astronauts placed some mirrors on the lunar surface. When the astronauts left, not only did they leave a flag and a lot of footprints, but also they left the means by which scientists back on Earth could bounce a beam of light off the Moon and capture the reflection.

Not just any mirror would work in this situation. The Moon's distance from Earth averages about 248,000 miles (400,000 km), and Earth is not much bigger in the Moon's sky than the Moon appears in the Earth's sky. Imagine aiming a mirror so that a narrow beam of light bounces off at precisely the right angle to return to the source. This would not be difficult to do if the source was across the room, but when the distance is several hundred thousand miles, such a feat is not possible. The beam would hit an ordinary mirror and reflect in a direction that would be unlikely to take it anywhere close to where it was needed.

Instead of ordinary mirrors, the astronauts carried retroreflectors. These devices have three mirrors situated at right angles to each other; the positioning is similar to putting a flat mirror on the floor and each wall of a corner in a bedroom. The geometry of retroreflectors means that an incoming light beam gets reflected back in the direction from where it came; no aiming is required, thanks to the multiple, perpendicular mirrors. Bicycle reflectors often use retroreflectors; the headlights of a car bounce off them and return directly to the driver, making the bicyclist easier to see, because the light reflects back toward the car and driver instead of scattering randomly over a wide area.

The idea behind the lunar retroreflectors was to give scientists on Earth a way to measure precisely the distance to the Moon. Because the speed of light is known, this distance can be found by measuring the time a beam requires to make the trip: Send a beam through space, clock the time when the reflection returns, and calculate the

Astronaut Edwin "Buzz" Aldrin walks past scientific experimental equipment placed on the Moon. The retroreflector is slightly left of center in this picture, just beyond the package in the foreground (which monitored seismic waves). *(NASA/Neil A. Armstrong)*

distance. With the retroreflectors in place, this would be an easy process—if not for the fact that light disperses (spreads out).

The phenomenon of dispersion can easily be seen by shining a flashlight beam onto a wall or flat surface some distance away. The diameter of the flashlight is only a few inches but the diameter of the circle of light displayed on the wall is much larger. Rather than traveling in a tight beam, ordinary light spreads out. Over the course of 248,000 miles (400,000 km), a beam from even the brightest and most focused flashlight or searchlight from Earth would spread so

Light Amplification by Stimulated Emission of Radiation

Light shows properties of both waves, as discovered by Thomas Young and James Clerk Maxwell, and particles called photons, as proposed by Albert Einstein. While working on additional theories of light, Einstein realized that a coherent type of light could be created if a collection of energetic atoms duplicated a single photon over and over again. If a photon enters a cavity full of atoms that were ready to emit the same kind of photon, stimulated emission occurs—the photon stimulates the atoms to emit other, identical photons. This process is a kind of light amplification, because the original photon has been amplified many times during stimulated emission. Lasers take their name from this phenomenon.

At first, stimulated emission was successful only for low-energy radiation such as microwaves—masers (microwave amplification by stimulated emission of radiation). Light, being of a higher frequency and therefore possessing more energy, proved much harder to stimulate and amplify. But in 1960 Theodore H. Maiman at Hughes Research Laboratory in California built a laser made of ruby; less than one inch (2.5 cm) long and about a third of an inch (0.8 cm) in diameter, this low-power but effective device introduced amplification and stimulated emission into the domain of visible light.

Lasers work by enclosing a material, called the medium, in a cavity between two polished, reflective surfaces. The medium contains the atoms or molecules that emit the photons. Energy from some source such as an intense light invigorates the medium. As shown in the figure on page 67, a single photon in the cavity eventually grows to a large collection of photons, all with identical properties—they are in phase and move in the same direction.

The energy is needed because the particles of the medium must be kept in an excited (energetic) state. Substances normally exist in a low-energy state, where only a few atoms have enough energy to emit photons (unless the substance is heated, in which case it glows with incandescent light). The energy pumped into the medium results in a population inversion: Most of the particles are in an excited state rather than a low-energy state, an inversion of the typical situation.

An effective laser medium requires atoms or particles with at least three relatively stable states. The energy absorbed by the

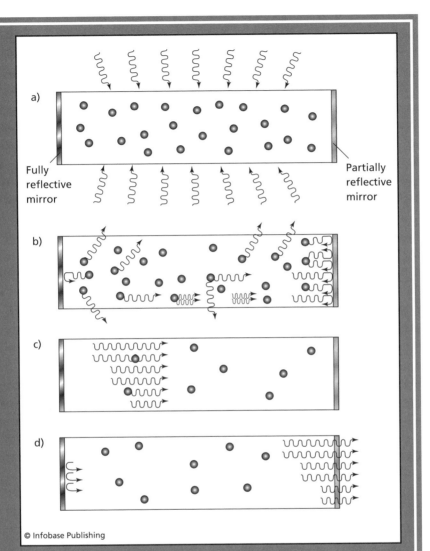

After absorbing energy, the atoms of a laser medium emit photons. Some of these photons escape; but a few bounce between the mirrors of the cavity, stimulating emission and becoming amplified. The resultant light is coherent.

medium knocks an electron from a low-energy (ground) state into a high-energy state, enabling the atom to emit light. But in a medium used for lasers, the atom needs another state, *(continued on next page)*

(continued from previous page)
possessing energy somewhere between the highest state and the ground state. The atoms emit a photon quickly to descend from the highest state to this middle state, called the upper laser state. (This low-energy photon is unimportant and escapes the container.) The upper laser state must be relatively stable, so the atom can reside there for a while; normally atoms will emit photons and reach ground quickly, but a laser medium is chosen to possess these stable, energetic states. The excited atoms dwell in the upper laser state until stimulated emission occurs; they are able to hold on to their energy for a period of time until a photon comes along and stimulates them. (Many lasers have four states, adding a "lower laser state," and stimulation of photons occurs between the two laser states.) Without at least one stable laser state, the atoms would simply flip-flop between the excited state and ground, absorbing and emitting photons instead of amplifying them.

The product of a laser is coherent light because the stimulated photons stay locked in step with each other, acting like a single "wave." The polished surfaces enclosing the laser medium act as mirrors, and the photons bounce back and forth until a sufficient number have accumulated. One of the surfaces is only a partial mirror, so eventually the amplified light can escape the cavity.

Lasers come in different varieties and get their names from the medium. Maiman's laser used ruby as the medium, but shortly afterward scientists developed many different kinds—gas, liquid, and solid. Each kind of laser has its own set of properties and is useful for certain applications, as described in the remaining sections of this chapter.

wide that only a few rays would strike the retroreflector. As a result, a vanishingly small number of rays would make the round trip, so the light bouncing from the retroreflector would be too feeble to detect.

What is needed to do this job is a source of light that does not disperse very much, or what is called *coherent light*. Lasers, first developed in 1960, generate this kind of light. The adjacent sidebar discusses lasers and the meaning behind the acronym composing their name.

Narrow beams of argon gas lasers made the journey to the Moon and spread out only to a diameter of about two miles (3.2 km); this is a tolerable dispersion and the retroreflectors returned enough light for scientists to detect. The successful experiment allowed scientists to calculate the distance between the Earth and the Moon to within four inches (10 cm), an accuracy of about one part in 4 million.

Distance measurements need not be confined to space. Geologists also use lasers for the precision monitoring of surfaces and structures on Earth. The San Andreas Fault, for example, is a fissure running along the west coast of California, created by two large "plates" of Earth's crust that are sliding past one another. This area is the site of many earthquakes. Geologists keep track of movements along this fault by a network of lasers and reflectors, and they can detect displacements of less than 0.04 inches (0.1 cm). Although monitoring these small movements will not necessarily predict the exact time of the next earthquake, these measurements inform geologists of the level of activity and whether it is increasing or decreasing.

The military uses laser range finders to calculate precise distances required for pinpoint artillery and bombing missions. *(United States Air Force/Master Sgt. Robert R. Hargreaves Jr.)*

The Lasers in CDs and DVDs

The coherent light from lasers has many uses besides measuring distances. A laser's narrow beam can read and write with remarkably tiny "letters."

The letters of a language need not be the same as those in English, German, or Spanish. Information-storage devices such as *compact discs* (CDs) use a series of pits and flat spaces to represent a binary language consisting of only two symbols, 0 and 1. The pits measure less than 0.00004 inches (0.0001 cm) in a CD and wind their way along the disc in a spiral track that, if stretched into a straight line, would be more than three miles (4.8 km) long. Computers and other digital machines use the binary language to store numbers and data encoding anything from an encyclopedia to a Beethoven symphony to a Britney Spears song.

One of the advantages of digital information is its accuracy—digital recordings of music, for example, do not have much noise introduced by unwanted signals or errors in the recording. The small size of the pits provides another advantage: The density of information is large. A computer CD can hold more than 450 times more data than floppy disks can, and they have replaced these formerly popular storage devices in many applications. By making the pits even smaller, DVDs store even more information—enough for an entire motion picture, though the movie must first be transformed into a special compressed format. (There is no agreement on what the acronym *DVD* stands for; some people claim it means Digital Video Disc, others say Digital Versatile Disc, and still others say it stands for nothing at all.) CDs and DVDs are currently the favorite storage medium for music and movies, sending the magnetic tape of cassettes and videotapes on their way to oblivion, just as cassettes did for the vinyl records of the 1950s and 1960s.

To read and write these information-rich discs requires a narrow, coherent beam of light. The pits are about the same size as the wavelength of light and are tightly packed along the spiral track, but lasers do a great job of concentrating light onto incredibly small areas. Lasers write CDs and DVDs by burning the pits into the aluminum substrate scaled into the plastic material of the discs. Reading the information requires shining a laser on the disc and measuring the reflection—the presence of a pit changes the reflectance, so the reader can determine whether there is a pit at any given location along the track.

Early CD players made use of small helium-neon gas lasers, but modern CD and DVD machines have a smaller, better laser, made from a semiconductor. A semiconductor is a material that normally does not carry an electric current but can be made to do so with the application of an electric field, by which the current can be controlled and switched on or off quickly and efficiently. Semiconductors such as germanium, gallium arsenide, and especially silicon are the basis for much of today's electronics industry because they form tiny but complex circuits. Semiconductors can also make lasers because under some conditions the electrons that carry the current fall into positively charged "holes" and emit light. This is the process by which light-emitting diodes (LEDs) work. But LEDs only provide ordinary, spontaneously emitted light; by constructing a semiconductor crystal such that photons pass back and forth through the material, stimulated emission can occur.

Semiconductor lasers can be as small as a grain of sand. Taking the place of mirrors are polished faces, or facets, of the crystal that keep the light confined until it is amplified. These tiny, low-power lasers have proven excellent for CD and DVD players as well as for barcode readers (devices that read codes represented by the black bars on the package of many consumer items) and laser pointers.

Another important application of semiconductor lasers involves communication. Thanks to the physics of light and a certain law of optics called *total internal reflection,* small strands of glass are magnificently effective message carriers.

Fiber Optics

The old way of transmitting voices from one telephone to another was to use copper wires. Telephones contain a microphone to turn the air-pressure waves (sound) that carry a voice into electrical signals, and a speaker that does the opposite, transforming the electrical signals back into air-pressure waves. The signals travel between the telephones of conversing people by copper wires, and networks operated by communications companies connect the right lines as the electrical signals passed from telephone to telephone.

But there is a better way to do the job. Light, especially a laser, is superior to electrical signals traveling along copper wires for a number of reasons, not the least of which is a huge difference in information capacity.

The frequency of a communication medium or signal limits the amount of information it can carry. A signal must change or vary in order to transmit information; a flat, unvarying line is not only boring—it also reveals very little information (rather like a book that consists of a single letter, *a*, repeated a million times). Messages containing information must use signals that vary over time, and higher-frequency signals have higher capacities. Visible light has a frequency millions of times greater than that of radio waves, and billions of times greater than that of the electrical signals carried by copper wires.

One of the problems with light as a message carrier is the same as the problem that stymied scientists who wanted to use light to measure distances—dispersion. The coherent light of lasers solved this problem, with the added benefits of being difficult to jam or intercept and less subject to interference. Since a tight beam of coherent light does not spread out, the receiver of a laser signal needs to be along the signal's path. And no one can listen in unless they are beamed the message, unlike radio messages.

But the narrowness of the beam also presents a difficulty. Communication between two telephone users means the beam must travel along the curvature of the planet's surface, possibly for a long distance. This requires some device or medium to "hold" the laser light in place, because light travels in a straight line. The medium must be transparent, relatively cheap, and flexible.

One way to keep the laser beam contained is in a tube lined with mirrors, but that turns out to be a poor solution. The trouble is that mirrors absorb a lot of light, turning the energy into a small amount of heat—an intolerable situation because the signal would fade quickly and fail to travel far.

The best way to confine a laser beam is to use the physics of light and a phenomenon, total internal reflection, which regulates the transmission of light from one medium to another. As discussed in chapter 2, when light encounters an interface between two different materials, some of it reflects and the rest passes through but refracts, or bends. When a ray of light travels from a material with a high index of refraction to a material with a lower one, the ray is bent away from the normal (perpendicular). But as shown in the figure below, if the light makes a large angle—in other words, if the ray barely grazes the interface—then all of it reflects. Beyond a certain angle called the critical angle, no transmission occurs; all light is reflected instead of just a portion. This is total internal reflection.

Glass has a higher refractive index than many other materials, including air, so light traveling inside glass cannot escape if it always strikes the interface at a greater than critical angle. Engineers design the glass fiber and the placement of tiny semiconductor lasers to accomplish this. The total diameter of fiber-optic cable is about the size of a human hair, although the core—the light-carrying glass—is only a tenth of this size. Surrounding the core

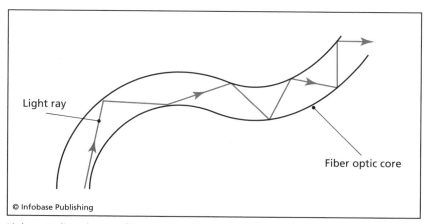

Light traveling down a fiber-optic cable strikes the edge at a large angle (with respect to the normal) and all of it reflects: total internal reflection.

is the cladding, a glassy material that has a lower index of refraction. An outer coating provides protection. Cables bundle together thousands of these tiny optical fibers, similar to a cable full of copper wires, though the fiber optics are much more efficient.

The semiconductor lasers are effective, but the glass must not absorb much light; otherwise, the same problem that plagued tubes with mirrored surfaces would ruin fiber optics. Making a highly transparent glass is not as easy as it sounds, because the light has to travel through miles of glass. Imagine a pane of glass as thick as a mile (1.6 km)—for most kinds of inexpensive window glass, little if any light would make it all the way through. But in 1970 researchers at the glass manufacturer Corning Glass Works solved the problem by making an extremely pure material that absorbs little light. (Impurities in glass are responsible for a great deal of light absorption.) The pure glass used for fiber optics is maximally transparent at frequencies in the infrared part of the spectrum, and because of this, the "light" traveling along fiber-optic cables is actually invisible infrared. In this portion of the spectrum, light can travel more than 50 miles (80 km) before it fades. By placing repeaters—semiconductor lasers that boost the signal—at these distances, the signal can travel as long as necessary to reach its destination.

One of the first businesses in the United States to install fiber optics for communications was Walt Disney World in Orlando, Florida, and in 1978 they linked their telephones, alarms, and light switches into a dense network of optical fibers. Because of its efficiency, one fiber-optic cable is worth several hundred copper wires, and so many other businesses followed Disney's lead. Ten years later a transatlantic cable, TAT-8, laid by the communications company AT&T, connected Europe and North America by fiber optics. Copper wires still exist, especially in homes, because of the expense of ripping out the wiring and replacing it, but today much of the information passing between computers linked to the Internet travels on fiber-optic cables. Companies like Corning and other manufacturers sold 30 billion dollars of fiber optics and associated equipment in 2002, in the expectation that copper wires will eventually become as quaint as stagecoaches.

Holography

The high frequency of light, along with the physics governing its emission by lasers, makes this part of the electromagnetic spectrum ideal for communication. Light not only transmits information; it can also be used to store and reproduce information, even if the information is an image of a three-dimensional figure.

The ordinary method of using light to store information is by taking a photograph. As discussed in chapter 2, a lens focuses light from a scene onto a photographic film, where a chemical reaction imprints the image. *Holography* is different. Instead of recording an image, the film records an interference pattern.

Interference is a common effect of the superposition of waves, as described in previous chapters. Soap films, discussed in chapter 3, display colors because of the interference of light reflecting from the inner and outer surfaces of the membrane. Interference involves the phase of a wave; waves that are out of phase (crest versus trough) cancel, and those that are in phase add to bigger amplitudes. Ordinary photographs merely record the amplitude of light (the brightness of each point) and, in color photography, the wavelengths. Holography adds phase information, a process that allows recovery of the original figure completely, including its three-dimensional features. Holography gets its name from the Greek words *holos*, meaning "complete," and *graphein*, "to write."

The coherent, monochromatic light of lasers is perfect for holography. As shown in the figure, the process involves splitting the laser beam into two parts (accomplished by a beam splitter that reflects one-half of the light and transmits the other half). One of the beams reflects from the object being recorded and strikes the film; the other beam takes a different route, avoiding the object but also striking the film. The two beams combine to produce an interference pattern—a complicated series of light and dark circles or stripes. Since lasers produce coherent radiation, the light begins the trips in phase, and the phase differences of the interference pattern on the film shows the different distances traveled by the two beams. If the distance is equal to exactly one wavelength (or some integer number of wavelengths), the two beams will arrive

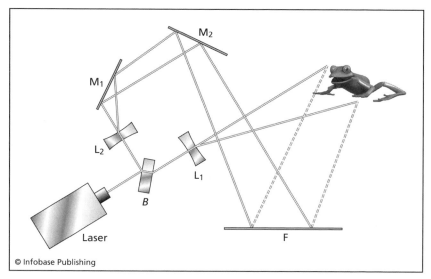

One holographic method splits laser light into two paths with a beam-splitter, B. Lenses L_1 and L_2 diverge the beams for better coverage. Mirrors M_1 and M_2 route one of the beams to bypass the object and strike the photographic film, F, whereas the other beam reflects from the object onto F. The photographic film records the pattern produced by wave interference.

at the film in phase and add constructively; otherwise, they will cancel to some extent. Holography generates three-dimensional figures because the phase information captures the distance of each point of the object.

The best way to view the resulting hologram is to face a beam of coherent light shining through the film. By changing the viewing angle, an observer can change the perspective—the figure appears to be in a different position, because the interference patterns contain all perspectives of the original scene. And since at each point the pattern holds information from every part of the scene, a small piece of the hologram is sufficient to reproduce the figure; but the piece is only capable of reproducing a small number of perspectives, so it can generate the figure only as seen from a certain angle.

Hungarian physicist Dennis Gabor discovered the theory behind holography in 1948 (for which he won the Nobel Prize in physics in 1971), and the first laser-generated holograms appeared in 1963, by Emmeth Leith and Juris Upatnieks. In the 1960s inventors developed holograms that can be viewed with ordinary (incoherent) light, allowing holography to decorate stamps and book covers. To produce these figures, a plastic film, imprinted with the interference pattern of the hologram, bends the light reflecting from a foil backing. This method, although crude, permits the manufacturing of millions of identical holograms. Since the images are not easy to produce, credit card companies often issue cards with security holograms in order to deter counterfeiters.

Holography is not just for making three-dimensional pictures. A Holographic Versatile Disc (HVD) is a data-storage instrument similar to a CD or DVD, but with a much larger information capacity. Although still in development, this promising technology offers a way to store 200 movies on a single disc, which is about 200 times the capacity of a DVD.

Current HVD techniques, researched and developed by a Tokyo-based company, Optware, involve two lasers of different colors (wavelengths). One laser writes the data as holographic-style interference patterns, while the other laser records formatting information to aid retrieval (similar to the file formatting of computer hard disks, CDs, and DVDs). The lasers are different wavelengths so that they can be separated. Another company, InPhase Technologies, Inc., of Longmont, Colorado, is working on HVD drives, similar to CD and DVD drives.

If HVDs live up to their potential, they will shrink the amount of space required to store almost any kind of information. A movie collection containing 200 DVDs, for example, fills several shelves today but would fit into a single small HVD disc. The text of all 29 million books of the United States Library of Congress could be stored in fewer than 10 of these discs.

Star Wars: The Strategic Defense Initiative

The coherency of laser light is useful for measurements, communications, and information storage, but the power of lasers motivates other applications. Per unit area, lasers can be brighter than the

Sun, and such energy is remarkably destructive when it is concentrated on a target for any length of time.

Destructive energy produced by powerful lasers can have important medical uses. *Laser-assisted In Situ Keratomileusis* (LASIK) is an eye surgery performed with lasers; the goal of the procedure is to correct vision problems by adjusting the shape of the patient's cornea. As mentioned in chapter 2, if the shape of a person's eyeball is slightly irregular, the cornea and lens may fail to focus the image on the retina. Eyeglasses and contact lenses can correct these problems, but another solution is to sculpt the cornea. *In situ* means the operation is performed with the eye in its normal position, and *keratomileusis* refers to the shaping of the corneal tissue. With the aid of a computer, the surgeon decides the best contour and applies a laser beam to sculpt the cornea. The laser used for these procedures usually has an ultraviolet beam.

LASIK surgery is not for everyone with vision problems. Only patients whose eyesight is relatively stable should opt for a LASIK or similar procedure. Laser eye surgeries are permanent, and if the person's eye and vision change afterward, the new shape will no longer be correct. Young people should wait, since growth and maturity commonly change the eyes and visual system. Most physicians will not perform LASIK on patients under 18 years of age.

But for older patients, LASIK offers the hope of reducing their dependence on eyeglasses or contact lenses. The surgery lasts only about 30 minutes and is a common procedure, with more than 1 million performed worldwide each year. Most procedures do not achieve perfect vision, but the surgery generally results in significant improvement.

LASIK procedures involve the use of a laser beam for controlled, precise vaporization of a small amount of tissue from a sedated patient. Achieving the desired shape requires computer control and precision mapping. The laser used is usually an excimer laser that generates radiation in the ultraviolet part of the spectrum (and is therefore invisible). The word *excimer* refers to an excited dimer—the energy pumped into the laser causes the chemicals in the medium to bind together, forming complexes called dimers.

The increase in the numbers of these excited dimers creates the population inversion required for stimulated emission. The high-power ultraviolet beam makes excimer lasers advantageous for eye surgeries such as LASIK.

Lasers can also be used in war. Many weapon systems already use lasers, although only for guidance—the beam is part of the apparatus instead of being the weapon itself. But the "death rays" of early science fiction stories are possible, in the form of high-power lasers. Although handheld laser weapons are not likely in the near future—they do not contain enough of the medium's material to generate powerful beams—powerful lasers exist. Among the strongest are CO_2 lasers that emit beams with a power of a billion *watts* or more, millions of times the power of the fastest car engines.

One of the most ambitious plans for the military use of lasers came to light when President Ronald Reagan made a speech in 1983 proposing the Strategic Defense Initiative (SDI). In the 1980s the cold war with the Soviet Union continued to rage, and President Reagan's idea was to use a variety of defensive weapons to intercept and defeat a possible nuclear attack.

A key element of SDI was a shield of protection created by satellite-based X-ray lasers. X-rays have high frequencies and therefore a tremendous amount of energy, useful for penetrating tissue during medical exams or, at high intensity, burning an enemy's missile. Using an array of satellite sensor systems to detect rocket launches, any missile launched by the Soviet Union would be intercepted and destroyed by high-power laser beams in midair, long before it reached United States soil.

The proposal became controversial for several reasons, including expense, practicality, and the effect such a system would have on already tense relations with the Soviet Union. Even at an estimated cost of more than 100 billion dollars, SDI would not have been guaranteed to work and would have required the development of new and unproved technologies. Satellites orbit Earth at speeds of thousands of miles per hour (otherwise they will fall to the ground), and missiles travel nearly as fast. Since both weapon and target are moving so quickly, achieving the precision needed for aiming would be difficult—according to some critics, impossible. Another concern was the reaction of the Soviet Union. No one knew if SDI would have caused them to spend billions of dollars improving their missiles or developing counteracting systems, possibly spreading the cold war into space.

In the end, SDI failed. Called "Star Wars" by some opponents—the name suggested that SDI was unattainable science fiction—the project cost the U.S. government 40 billion dollars in the 1980s and 1990s, but no missile defense system approaching that envisioned by President Reagan emerged.

But the goal has not been forgotten. The cold war is over but nuclear missiles remain, and now eight countries—the United States, the United Kingdom, France, England, Russia, Pakistan, India, and North Korea—claim to have nuclear capability. (Many people doubt North Korea's claim, but missiles may be lurking in regions of the world besides those listed above.) Today the National Missile Defense program of the United States military includes a proposal for an airborne laser (ABL), attached to a modified Boeing 747. Flying at about 40,000 feet (12,200 m), the airplane would consist of a tracking beam and a high-power laser. In a few seconds the million-watt laser beam could overheat and destroy a missile at a distance of hundreds of miles.

This ABL aircraft is a modified 747 carrying a powerful laser, the beam of which exits from the plane's nose. *(Missile Defense Agency)*

The present design for ABL uses a chemical oxygen iodine laser, in which a reaction between chlorine and other chemicals—hydrogen peroxide and potassium hydroxide—provides energy to iodine atoms, by way of oxygen atoms. The excited iodine generates infrared radiation, which is not as strong as X-rays but when concentrated can be every bit as effective a weapon. The ABL is still in its test phase, but the hope is that the system will become operational by 2008.

Traveling by Laser

Lasers focus the energy of light into a narrow, concentrated beam—this is how lasers can vaporize tissue or overheat missiles. But this concentrated energy can also generate propulsion.

In 2003, *National Aeronautics and Space Administration* (NASA) scientists at the Marshall Space Flight Center in Huntsville, Alabama, kept an airplane with a five-foot (1.5-m) wingspan aloft by shining a laser on it. Energy cells on board the airplane converted the light into the energy needed to rotate the propeller. The vehi-

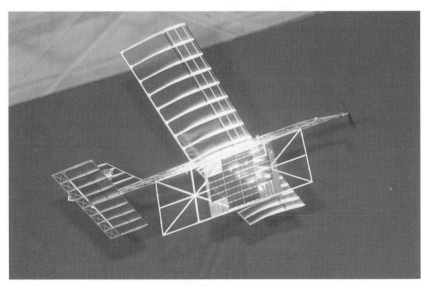

A laser maintains its beam on this lightweight airplane, providing the energy to keep it aloft inside a hanger at NASA's Marshall Space Flight Center in Huntsville, Alabama, on September 18, 2003. *(NASA/Tom Tschida)*

cle, weighing less than a pound, could remain in the air as long as the laser maintained an uninterrupted beam on the cells. This technology, when fully developed, would permit flights of indefinite duration by airplanes with no need for fuel, providing more room for passengers or equipment. Chapter 9 examines in more detail the use of the energy of light.

Light propulsion can also be generated by explosions. Most automobiles and airplanes today move under the force created by fuel exploding in internal combustion engines. The burning of this fuel liberates a large quantity of energy, sufficient to push a piston or rotate a turbine. A high-power laser beam can also produce heating and explosions. The advantage of using a laser to generate an explosion is that the fuel can be cheap and lightweight, such as air; the energy comes from the light, not chemicals in the fuel. Weight is a huge factor in space launches because of the expense of accelerating a heavy rocket, plus its fuel, up to escape velocity. Any reduction in weight is beneficial.

Lightcraft Technologies, Inc., a company based in Vermont, has already tested several small light-propelled vessels in the desert of New Mexico. A ground-based CO_2 laser supplies the light, and mirrors on the vessel itself route the beam and focus it on the fuel. The engine produces thrust in the same way that a conventional, chemical rocket does—because of Newton's third law, which says that every action has an equal and opposite reaction. The heated fuel spews out of the back, and the vessel moves forward, propelled by the power of light.

Contrary to science fiction movies, lasers—even ones that make visible light—cannot be seen in space (unless the beam of a certain intensity and visibility happens to strike the eye of the observer). In air, lasers that operate in the visible portion of the spectrum can be seen for the same reason that rays streaming in from a window can: Dust particles reflect some of the beam toward the eye. In space there is little to reflect the light, and so the fantastic space battles depicted in Hollywood movies, with dancing beams of light striking ship after ship, are impossible.

But the idea of lasers in space, as agents of both destruction and propulsion, is not at all far-fetched. Today, lasers reach out and bounce off the Moon as easily as they melt away tissue to shape corneas and travel along glass fibers the diameter of a human hair. Tomorrow these amazing sources of coherent light might propel an airplane or even a rocket.

5

LIGHT'S SERVICE TO LIFE AND MEDICINE

L IGHT IS VITAL for life on Earth. One of light's most prominent contributions is vision—as discussed in chapter 2, the absorption of light by the eye gets turned into signals that, when properly interpreted by the brain, provide a rich amount of information about the world. Vision allows an organism to sense objects at a distance, which is important for detecting potential food or predators, and which helps in moving quickly and gracefully through the environment.

But light plays many other critical roles for life on this planet:

♦ Light is energy, and sunlight offers an abundant and freely available resource.

♦ Plants use sunlight to make the energy-rich molecules that are the foundation of Earth's food chain.

♦ Humans harness the energy of light indirectly—by eating plants—and in more direct ways to advance technology and medical procedures.

Light is so important that humans and animals have learned to make use of whatever light is available, even if it is not visible to the eye. Some animals have even developed an ability to make light all on their own.

Glowing in the Dark

The flashing lights hovering over a lawn on a summer evening are one of nature's most fascinating spectacles. The lights come from the glowing abdomens (rear segments) of fireflies and are a form of communication—the insects are looking for mates.

Fireflies belong to the family *Lampyridae,* and there are about 2,000 species of these flying insects. One of the most common fireflies in North America, the Pyralis firefly, is less than an inch (2.5 cm) long and emits a greenish yellow glow. Both males and females in most species can glow, although with different patterns. Different species also have different patterns, so that the members of one species can recognize each other and distinguish between their own and other species. The Pyralis males fly around emitting a continuous, five-second light, and a female, if interested, will respond with a shorter flash of light.

Other animals besides fireflies can glow, although most animals that show *bioluminescence*—the emission of light by living organisms—live in the sea. Some species of jellyfish are bioluminescent,

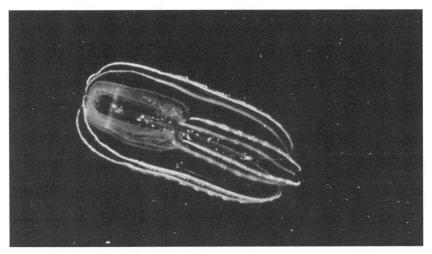

This marine animal, called a ctenophore, is bioluminescent. *(NOAA/OAR/NURP)*

and so are many deep-sea fish, which live so far below the surface that little sunlight reaches them. Deep-sea animals often produce their own light so that they can hunt or attract prey.

Bioluminescence is different from the glow of a lightbulb, which is called incandescence. Incandescence is an emission of light due to heating, such as the glow of a bulb's filament heated by the flow of electricity through it, whereas bioluminescence is a "cold" light coming from chemical reactions. Bioluminescence is also not the same as fluorescence and phosphorescence, since these two phenomena produce light by the reemission of light that was absorbed earlier.

The chemical reactions of bioluminescence involve the oxidation (combining with oxygen) of molecules called luciferin. This reaction occurs slowly and does not happen fast enough to emit a noticeable

Luciferase: An Illuminating Enzyme

Luciferase gets its name from the Latin word *lucifer*, which means light-bearer, and refers to a class of enzymes (there are several different types of luciferase). But all these enzymes catalyze (speed up) a reaction involving the combination of oxygen with luciferin (of which there are also several different types). The basic reaction produces light and heat:

luciferin + oxygen —> light + heat

Another molecule, called *adenosine triphosphate* (*ATP*), is necessary in many cases. ATP is a molecule that provides the cells and tissues of an organism with a source of energy, like a fuel, because this molecule drives many of the reactions needed to maintain life. In fireflies, for example, luciferase requires ATP to catalyze the oxidation of luciferin.

Fireflies and other bioluminescent organisms want to produce light instead of heat, and the reaction catalyzed by luciferase is effective because it yields much more light than heat. Unlike an incandescent lightbulb, which wastes more than 90 percent of its energy as heat, only a few percent of the energy of the luciferin reaction is lost as heat. This is why a lightbulb gets hot but the abdomen of a firefly does not.

Luciferase does not need to be inside a living organism to work, since it will produce light anywhere there is oxygen and light except in the presence of an enzyme called luciferase. Luciferase speeds up the reaction so that it produces a visible quantity of light—and the firefly glows. But luciferase will work outside of a firefly as well as inside, and people use this amazing enzyme for a variety of purposes, as discussed in the sidebar on page 86.

The number of organisms that glow in the dark has recently increased due to the ability of biologists to transfer genes between different species. Transgenic animals—animals whose genetic material has been altered by transferring genes—include aquarium fish that glow in the dark because they have a gene, normally found in marine animals such as jellyfish or sea anemone, which makes a fluorescent protein. This is not the same as the bioluminescence discussed above because the protein reemits absorbed light instead of catalyzing a chemical reaction, but the effect is

luciferin (and ATP, if required). Medical personnel sometimes use luciferase to check blood supplies. Hospitals store blood for use as needed, but if the blood is old then some of the components, such as red blood cells, may begin to rupture, which makes the blood unusable. Since red blood cells contain ATP, this molecule leaks out of ruptured cells, and when it is exposed to luciferin and luciferase the fluid will glow. If a blood sample glows in the dark when tested under these conditions, it is too old for use.

Scientists use luciferase and light as a way to check their genetic experiments. These experiments sometimes involve transferring a gene into an organism, but it is usually difficult to tell if the gene was successfully transferred or not. The experimenter will often transfer another gene—a "reporter" gene—at the same time and use the reporter gene to indicate success. The gene that makes luciferase is a good reporter gene because if it is present and functional, the tissue will emit light upon the addition of luciferin (and oxygen and ATP, if required, although these substances are present in most tissues already). If the gene transfer was successful, the organism or some part of its tissues will glow in the dark! For example, when scientists at the University of California, Los Angeles, wanted to track genes inserted in the muscles of mice, they used firefly luciferase.

similar—a glowing organism. Taikong, a company in Taiwan, and an American company, Yorktown Technologies, began to sell glowing fish in 2003.

Turning Light into Food

Animals use light to attract mates or prey—or it can attract buyers of unusually glowing fish—but plants and some types of bacteria use light for another purpose. They convert sunlight into molecules rich in energy—food. This process is called photosynthesis.

Photosynthesis is the opposite of using energy to create light. Bioluminescence results in the breakdown of molecules (luciferin, and in many cases ATP) to yield energy in the form of light, plus a little heat. Photosynthesis occurs when plants synthesize, or make, molecules with the aid of energy coming from sunlight. The process begins when a molecule in the plant called chlorophyll absorbs light.

Chapter 1 discussed atoms and molecules and their emission of light, which happens when an electron falls from a higher-energy orbit to a lower one. The absorption of light has the opposite result, bumping electrons into high-energy orbits. One of three things usually happens to the energy after absorption:

♦ It may get reemitted later (as in fluorescence).

♦ It may get passed along to other molecules.

♦ It may trigger chemical reactions.

What happens in the photosynthetic process is a series of steps in which the energy sometimes gets passed along to other molecules and sometimes triggers chemical reactions.

The color of objects, as described in chapter 3, comes from the wavelength of light reflected by the object. The leaves of plants are green because they reflect a great deal of light from the middle part of the visible spectrum, which to the human eye appears green, and then absorb a lot of light from either end of the spectrum (red and blue). The reason for this is the absorption spectrum of chlorophyll, which absorbs red and blue light much more readily than green.

The absorption of a photon takes an astonishingly short time, roughly 10^{-15} seconds. The captured energy initiates a series of reactions involving numerous molecules catalyzed by enzymes, all of which can be summarized in the following formula:

$$6CO_2 + 6H_2O \text{ (and light)} \rightarrow C_6H_{12}O_6 + 6O_2.$$

The end result is that six molecules of carbon dioxide (CO_2) and six molecules of water (H_2O) get transformed into a molecule of glucose ($C_6H_{12}O_6$) and six molecules of oxygen (O_2). Plants take carbon dioxide and water and, with the energy from light, convert them into an energy-rich molecule, glucose, plus oxygen.

Animals are unable to make glucose, so they must consume plants—or other animals—in order to obtain fuel for their bodies. Glucose is a carbohydrate, as suggested by the formula $C_6H_{12}O_6$, which can be rewritten as $6(CH_2O)$—carbon plus water, or in other words a hydrate (water) of carbon. Animals and many single-celled organisms use glucose in a series of reactions called respiration, summarized by the following formula:

$$C_6H_{12}O_6 + 6O_2 \rightarrow 6CO_2 + 6H_2O \text{ (and energy}$$
$$\text{to make ATP molecules).}$$

Plants use carbon dioxide to make food and release oxygen, and animals "burn" food with oxygen to retrieve the stored energy and make molecules of ATP, which provide energy for the maintenance, repair, and daily chores of living tissues. Carbon dioxide and water return to the environment, exhaled by the animal. The cycle, begun with plant photosynthesis and ending with animal respiration, relies entirely on sunlight. Without light there could be no life, at least not in its present form.

Biological Clocks and Light

Although animals cannot use light to make food, they can use it to set their internal clocks. Many of the activities of both plants and animals are rhythmic, occurring periodically, and the period of these rhythms is often a day. One of the most obvious of these daily rhythms is the sleep-wake cycle: Most people (except those who work nights) go to sleep at night and are active during the day. Some species of animals, such as mice, do the opposite. Other rhythms include the fluctuation of body temperature, hormones, and, for plants, leaf movements and the reactions involved in photosynthesis. The molecule melatonin, rhythmically secreted by a gland in the brain called the pineal gland, controls the rhythms of many animals, including humans. Rhythms with a period of about 24 hours are called circadian rhythms, after the Latin words *circa* (around) and *dies* (day).

Earth's approximate 24-hour rotation—resulting in one day and night—provides a relatively constant clock, and in ancient civilizations was the timekeeper. The daily rhythm of light and dark is also an effective signal for plant and animal tissues to set their circadian rhythms, and they certainly make use of this signal. But sunlight does not create a circadian rhythm in animals and people, because many living organisms have an internal clock that is independent of day and night. This clock is continually running, but does not quite have a 24-hour period.

The internal clock becomes evident when people live for an extended time in the absence of sunlight. French geologist Michel Siffre volunteered to spend several months isolated in a cave in Texas in 1972, and scientists studied his body's rhythms, including sleep-wake activity. This and similar experiments showed that people in isolation continue to have circadian rhythms, but the period of these rhythms averages about 25 hours, slightly longer than a day. What sunlight does is entrain these rhythms, so in the normal situation all the body's rhythms are synchronized and occur at the right time. Without periodic light the body's activities sometimes get out of step, resulting in sleep disturbances or other problems.

NASA was one of the organizations sponsoring the Siffre experiment. The American space agency studies circadian rhythms because astronauts often experience conditions in which these rhythms may be upset. Space shuttle astronauts orbit the Earth every 90 minutes, and their "day" lasts only about 45 minutes, which can disrupt the body's clock. The disruptions can cause physiological problems and slow a person's performance—a dangerous situation for an astronaut in space, who may have to respond to any number of emergencies.

A similar problem occurs when people travel across several time zones, a phenomenon known as jet lag. A New York resident who flies to London experiences a time of change of five or occasionally six hours (depending on Daylight Savings Time). If the traveler's normal bedtime is 10:00 P.M., the internal clock may cause him or her a sleepless night until about 3:00 or 4:00 A.M. in London, which corresponds to the end of the day in New York.

Jet lag wears off after exposure to sunlight gradually entrains the traveler's circadian rhythm to match the new time zone. Some people try to "reset" their clock in advance by swallowing melatonin pills in order to match their rhythm to the time zone into which they will be traveling. NASA sometimes exposes astronauts who are about to embark on a mission to bright artificial lights in order to guide their circadian rhythms, since it is extremely important that the astronauts be wide awake and at maximum efficiency during liftoff, no matter what time of day or night this occurs.

Finding Prey in the Dark

Light not only offers a source of energy and a means to train circadian rhythms but also provides the information needed for vision, as discussed in chapter 2. People cannot see in the dark.

But what constitutes visible light depends on the species of the observer. Electromagnetic radiation that humans call visible light is only a small portion of the whole spectrum. The lowest frequency humans can see is reddish light—people perceive this light as red in color—and just beneath this range, with a slightly lower frequency, lies infrared radiation. This radiation, described in more detail in chapter 6, is important because all warm objects emit a lot of infrared radiation. Infrared, with its smaller wavelength and lower frequency, has slightly less energy than visible light. While hot objects such as incandescent bulbs have enough energy to glow with visible light, warm objects only have enough energy to emit infrared.

Although humans cannot see infrared, members of the pit viper family of snakes can. Pit vipers include rattlesnakes, a type of poisonous snake that feeds on birds and small mammals and is common in many parts of the United States. Objects emitting large quantities of infrared include the bodies of living people and animals, which explains why a rattlesnake can strike with deadly accuracy even well after the Sun has gone down.

Imagine a mouse scurrying around in the dark, active at night because most predators cannot see. But the mouse's body temperature is perhaps 20°F (11.1°C) hotter than its surroundings. Objects at warmer temperatures emit more radiation, and a pit viper has two infrared sensors located in pits at the side of its face that are so sensitive they can detect temperature differences of about 0.0036°F (0.002°C). To the snake, the mouse stands out like the beacon of a lighthouse.

Goggles worn by soldiers at night sometimes also consist of infrared detectors. Some of these night-vision devices amplify visible light, but other instruments make use of the more abundant infrared radiation. Anything warmer than its background emits more infrared radiation, and short of lowering temperature there is little that can be done to hide from an infrared detector.

Laser Surgery

Infrared radiation is slightly beneath the red portion of visible light. Slightly beyond the other end of the spectrum—the blue or violet wavelengths—there is ultraviolet radiation. Ultraviolet has a higher frequency than the highest frequency of light that people can detect.

Since the energy of electromagnetic radiation is proportional to its frequency, ultraviolet radiation has a little more energy than visible light. This makes ultraviolet a little more dangerous, though sometimes a little more useful. Eye doctors use ultraviolet to sculpt the cornea of eyes and improve faulty vision.

Lasers, the subject of chapter 4, generate coherent, intense beams of electromagnetic radiation. Radiation of any frequency can be powerful (and dangerous) when it comes from a laser, and surgeons sometimes perform cutting operations with lasers instead of knives or scalpels. The advantages of the laser are its ease of control, which allows surgeons to make a precise incision, and also the heat produced by a laser beam, which seals off broken blood vessels so there is not as much bleeding. The heat can also be used to burn off tissue, a function required for many cosmetic operations as well as laser eye surgery.

Chapter 2 discussed human vision and how the cornea and lens combine to refract light and focus an image on the retina, at the back of the eye. Because of its size and composition, the cornea does most of the bending, while tiny muscles adjust the shape of the lens for fine-tuning. But the cornea is not the right shape or the eyeball is too long or too short in many people, and the visual system cannot adjust for these flaws. Vision in these people is blurry unless they wear eyeglasses or contact lenses to focus the image properly.

Lenses compensate for too much or too little bending by the cornea, but another method of correcting vision is to correct the eye itself, shaping the cornea to the right dimensions for a person's eyeball. A cornea of the precise thickness and geometry would create a clearer image on the retina. Although surgeons have performed this kind of surgery with sharp knives, lasers offer much superior tools for this job. A common procedure is LASIK (Laser-assisted In Situ Keratomileusis), as discussed in chapter 3.

Seeing through Skin

Surgery is not a gentle procedure. Although cutting or burning tissue is often medically necessary and, with modern medicine, carries only a small or moderate risk of infection, both patient and doctor would usually prefer a less invasive procedure. Physicians study bones and other internal structures with X-rays—high-frequency electromagnetic radiation discussed in chapter 6—and avoid having to cut open the skin in many circumstances. Infrared light also gives a window into the body, although it delivers a much different picture.

Transparency creates windows. A glass window lets light into a room because it is transparent to electromagnetic radiation in the frequency range of visible light. Most tissues of the human body are transparent to electromagnetic radiation known as near infrared—frequencies just barely below the red portion of the visible light spectrum. (This ranger is called "near" because it is so near in frequency and wavelength to visible light.) Near-infrared radiation can pass through the body, including the bones.

The window provided by near infrared is a relatively recent discovery. Scientist Frans Jöbsis asked his 14-year-old son Paul to clean a thin chuck roast bone in 1976, and when the boy held it up to the light, they noticed that a small amount of red light passed through it. Jöbsis suspected that if red light penetrated the bone then near infrared, with its longer wavelength, might work better.

Although the body allows passage of near infrared, there are important interactions—near infrared does not zip through as if the body were not there. As discussed in the sidebar "Absorption and Emission Spectrum" in chapter 1, atoms and molecules often absorb and reemit radiation, and this process provides clues to the nature of the material. The same is true for near infrared's travels through the human body.

Jöbsis realized that near infrared could be used to gain information about the state and health of internal tissue—even tissue such as the brain that is normally well hidden by the skull. Jöbsis published a paper in *Science* in 1977 titled "Noninvasive, Infrared Monitoring of Cerebral and Myocardial Oxygen Sufficiency and Circulatory Parameters," in which he identified a procedure to monitor the oxygen level of brain (cerebral) and heart (myocardial) tissue. Jöbsis used absorption bands caused by molecules in the blood—hemoglobin and an enzyme known as cytochrome oxidase—to determine the oxygen level, because when these molecules bind to oxygen they have a different absorption pattern.

Oxygen is essential for respiration and its concentration tends to change in active tissues. This is particularly true in the brain, in which the oxygen situation changes where there is activity corresponding to voluntary movement, such as when a person waves a hand or kicks a football, or activity due to thought or concentration. These changes give scientists and physicians insight into the brain at work, and they can be monitored by expensive machines such as magnetic resonance imaging (MRI). In the 1990s, Britton Chance, an investigator at the University of Pennsylvania, sent short pulses of near infrared through the brain of animals and, later, human volunteers, measuring the blood oxygen dynamics. Although the much simpler near-infrared devices do not offer the same amount of information provided by MRI, they can help determine what part of the brain does what, and when.

Future Medical Uses of Light

Light of all colors and intensities is a part of medicine today, but near infrared has a great potential for expanding its role. Two recent developments reinforce the promise offered by this excellent window into the body.

Britton Chance, professor emeritus at the University of Pennsylvania, and Banu Onaral, director of Drexel University's School of Biomedical Engineering, Science, and Health Systems, have been working on a tool to help with the early diagnosis of breast cancer. This disease strikes more than a quarter of a million women in the United States per year, and the prognosis is far better when physicians detect the cancer in its early stages. Self-examination and procedures such as a mammogram are important for detecting breast cancer and will continue to remain so, but Chance, Onaral, and their colleagues have developed a handheld scanner that might soon assist in identifying women who may need to seek medical attention.

The instrument uses near infrared to examine the tissue. Cancers arise from uncontrolled growth, a process that requires an extra amount of nutrients and oxygen. Blood supplies the needed substances, and abnormal growths such as tumors must have additional blood vessels to nourish them. This excess activity causes small changes in temperature and blood oxygen levels, which can be detected by equipment such as the scanner designed by

Chance, Onaral, and colleagues. The simple and portable scanner beeps to alert the user of the results. Tests indicate an accuracy of better than 90 percent.

Another promising device using near infrared could offer a simple method of monitoring brain oxygen levels during surgery. Patients undergoing heart operations are especially susceptible to impairments in circulation leading to oxygen deprivation of the brain, an organ that can tolerate a loss of oxygen for only very short periods of time. Prolonged loss causes tissue damage and can lead to a disability in movement, speech, memory, or thinking processes.

Existing instruments to determine brain oxygen levels during surgery often rely on measurements of the blood in other parts of the body, providing an indirect measurement. Most of the methods are also invasive and introduce some risk of infection. Researchers at Duke University Medical Center, led by anesthesiologist David MacLeod, have used a new device called a cerebral oximeter that monitors brain oxygen levels with near infrared. The cerebral oximeter has a laser to send a safe, low-intensity beam of near infrared through the patient's skull, and sensors attached to the head measure the scattered light. Because of the absorption characteristics mentioned earlier, the measurements reveal oxygen levels in the brain quickly and directly.

By traveling where ordinary light cannot go, near infrared provides pictures of otherwise dark and concealed places. Radiation at or near the frequency of visible light is so strongly tied to life that this comes as no surprise. Abundant sunshine was an early stimulus for plants to develop photosynthesis and animals to develop vision, and light became so important that some animals carry their own technique for making it—bioluminescence—or use whatever frequency is available, like the infrared sensors of a pit viper. Light is both illuminating and nourishing to all life on the planet.

6

ELECTROMAGNETIC RADIATION AND THE UNIVERSE

THE NIGHT SKY appears dark, particularly on a night without moonlight when the only visible objects are a few planets and the stars—little points of light. People who live away from the bright lights of big cities can see a few thousand stars in their night sky, but starlight is so dim that the background light of the city outshines and obscures all except a few dozen of the nearest and brightest stars. This is a tiny subset of the approximately 300 billion stars in the galaxy.

But the night sky is dark only to human eyes—the universe is awash in electromagnetic radiation. Some of this radiation escapes notice because it is so dim and distant, and some of it fails to be detected by the human eye because it is not in the frequency range of visible light. Coming from all directions are a vast number of electromagnetic waves of many different frequencies from a variety of sources, invisible to the human eye but not to the sensitive instruments of astronomers and physicists.

The same principles governing visible light also hold true for electromagnetic radiation of other frequencies. The speed, for instance, is the same for all electromagnetic radiation traveling through a vacuum—186,200 miles/second (300,000 km/s). But as mentioned numerous times throughout this book, the energy of radiation depends on its frequency and wavelength, and the various frequencies have their own special properties. Similar to the way that vision provides a tremendous quantity of information about the world, observing the whole spectrum of electromagnetic waves is an expanded form of vision that reveals much about the nature of the universe.

Radio Waves

In 1886, German physicist Heinrich Hertz (1857–94) invented simple devices to make and detect nonvisible electromagnetic waves. He produced these waves with a spark discharge, and detected them with a receiver consisting of a loop of wire. The waves traveled only a few yards but the experiment was a great success. These waves, called radio waves, had the same properties of light, including velocity, reflection, and refraction, and Hertz realized that radio waves belonged in the same class of radiation. As mentioned in chapter 1, Scottish physicist James Clerk Maxwell had already proposed the existence of electromagnetic radiation and the idea that light is an example of this type of radiation. Hertz's experiment supported Maxwell's theories.

Radio waves take their name from the popular news and entertainment medium that uses these waves. Radio waves are electromagnetic radiation of the lowest frequency and longest wavelength, which means that they have the lowest energy. Any electromagnetic wave with a wavelength of about a foot (30 cm) or more is a radio wave, and some radio waves are so enormous that a single cycle stretches for more than a mile (1.6 km)!

Although radio waves take their name from radio—one of their earliest uses—today these waves carry television programs and cell phone conversations as well. The low energy of this radiation means that even though people live in a world bombarded by radio transmissions and broadcasts, no harm is done. The use of radio waves in communication is the subject of chapter 7.

With so many radio frequencies and channels in use, inter-ference can become a problem. Even in the early days of radio, people worried about other sources of radio waves and how they might affect transmissions. In the late 1920s and early 1930s Bell Telephone Laboratories began studying the possibility of radio communication across the Atlantic Ocean, and they hired Karl Jansky (1905–50) to investigate sources of radio waves that could interfere with these transmissions. Jansky made an *antenna* tuned to a frequency of about 20.5 million hertz, corresponding to a wavelength of about 47.6 feet (14.5 m), and he mounted it on a rotating support so that it could be turned in any direction.

Jansky found several sources of potential interference. Thun-derstorms created some of the strongest signals, a vexing problem for communication since these weather systems are not control-lable or predictable. Another source was a weak but constant hiss, more mysterious than thunderstorms because at first Jansky could not figure out what or where it was. Jansky finally pinpointed the origin after months of work—these waves were coming from the sky and were quite strong in the direction of the center of the Milky Way.

Radio Astronomy—Viewing the Universe with Radio

Jansky's discovery was the birth of radio astronomy. Scientists real-ized that radio wave signals from astronomical bodies gave them another way to study these distant objects, and they built radio telescopes to "listen" to the solar system, stars, and galaxies.

Radio astronomers do not really listen to these transmissions; rather, they treat radio wave signals in a manner similar to how they treat light. The radio waves strike an array of sensitive receiv-ers, and astronomers use the data to make a picture or an image, much as a camera produces a picture when light falls onto photo-graphic film. The images are "radio snapshots" of the source.

Many objects in the universe emit radio waves, including planets, stars, and clouds of sparse gas distributed throughout space. Solar flares—sudden outbursts from small areas of the Sun—are powerful emitters of radio waves, sometimes strong enough to disrupt radio communication on Earth, but most of the signals from astronomical radio sources are faint. Even though they are weak, radio waves in astronomy offer at least one advantage over light, because many radio wavelengths easily pass through the gas, dust, and clouds of the atmosphere. Overcast skies hamper astronomers who study light but have much less effect on those who study radio waves.

Radio telescopes are similar to other instruments designed to detect and receive electromagnetic radiation. Incoming radio waves bounce off a dish-shaped reflector, which focuses the waves onto a conductor or an antenna in the central point. The electromagnetic waves induce a tiny but detectable current in the conductor, and

The radio telescope in the foreground is 230 feet (70 m) in diameter and is located at Goldstone, California, in the Mojave Desert. NASA uses this instrument to make astronomical observations as well as to communicate with spacecraft and probes. *(NASA-JPL)*

sensitive electronic equipment amplifies this current to boost the signal. In order to capture as much radiation as possible, the reflector is large, just like the light-based reflecting telescopes discussed in chapter 2. A benefit of the longer wavelengths of radio waves is that radio reflectors need not be as smooth as those designed for visible light; mirrors distort reflected waves if the surface has bumps as big as or bigger than the wavelength, so mirrors for light must have a much more finely polished surface than a "mirror" for radio waves.

But there is a disadvantage of radio's longer wavelength. Because a radio wave is so long it does not give as much detail as a wave of light. As described in chapter 2, optical instruments have limited resolution—they cannot distinguish extremely small objects. The resolution of an instrument depends on the wavelength it uses, and smaller wavelengths provide better resolution. The enormous wavelengths of radio waves mean that radio telescopes cannot pinpoint sources in the sky as well as a light-based telescope of the same size. To give adequate resolution, radio telescopes must be much larger than their light-based cousins.

Even though radio telescopes do not have to be as smooth as other telescopes, their size is limited because a dish cannot be so massive that it is unmovable or unusable. But astronomers extend the range by borrowing a technique from optics called interferometry. As discussed in chapter 3, an interferometer uses wave interference to make measurements. When waves such as light or radio travel different distances to the same point, they may interfere with or cancel one another because they arrive out of phase (at different points in their cycle). For instance, when a wave at its crest encounters a similar sized wave at its trough, the amplitude of the combination is zero. Radio astronomers use interferometry by combining the signals of separate receivers, which produces interference bands of varying amplitude in the same way that light does (though on a broader scale because of radio's larger wavelength). These interference bands change over time because the Earth rotates, and astronomers who study these bands and how they change can obtain a crisper "radio" picture of the sky.

One of the world's most sensitive radio observatories uses inter-ferometry in this manner. The Very Large Array (VLA), located on a flat plain about 50 miles (80 km) west of Socorro, New Mexico, consists of 27 radio antennas arranged in a Y shape. Each antenna has a reflecting dish 82 feet (25 m) in diameter, attached to a mov-able mount. The distance between antennas is adjustable, and at maximum separation, interferometry can give these receivers a combined resolution similar to an antenna of 22 miles (36 km). This resolution gives the telescope the ability to see a radio source the size of a golf ball at a distance of about 100 miles (160 km).

Astronomers have used radio telescopes for many types of observation. The study of radio waves from the Sun has given astronomers a great deal of information about the violent activi-ties on the surface, including sudden eruptions, such as flares, that can disrupt communication and damage satellites. Radio tele-scopes also provide information about the surfaces of the planets, including surface temperatures and the nature of storms such as those swirling around in Jupiter's atmosphere. With the help of spectrum-analyzing equipment, radio observations have enabled astronomers to find such compounds as carbon dioxide, water vapor, and ethanol (alcohol) in space. VLA has been a big part of these efforts and has made many contributions since its formal dedication in 1980. Astronomer David Wilner of the Harvard-Smithsonian Center for Astrophysics recently used VLA to exam-ine a planetary system in the making. Wilner observed the star system named TW Hydrae and observed a disk of at least a billion miles (1.6 billion km) full of pebbles and rocks that one day might form planets as they collide and adhere.

While VLA extends its resolution by using multiple dishes, some radio observatories consist of a single, large dish. The larg-est single-dish radio telescope is the Arecibo Observatory, located in Puerto Rico. The huge diameter of the Arecibo telescope spans 1,000 feet (305 m)—more than three American football fields—and contains nearly 40,000 aluminum panels. Astronomers work-ing at Arecibo have made numerous exciting findings, including the 1991 discovery by Alex Wolszczan and his colleagues of the first planet beyond the solar system. This discovery touched off a frenzy of *extrasolar planet* searches, and as of late 2006 about 200 have been discovered.

The existence of planets orbiting other stars makes some people wonder if life may have arisen elsewhere in the galaxy, as it did on Earth. If so, other civilizations may have evolved, and these civilizations would probably develop sciences and technologies similar to those of humans on Earth, since the laws and principles of physics and other sciences should hold true throughout the universe. In particular, these other civilizations may be using radio waves to communicate, as people do on Earth. To search for signs of these extraterrestrial (beyond Earth) civilizations, radio astronomers have trained their telescopes on numerous stars, looking for radio signals with regular or repeating patterns indicating some sort of message. The first search, by astronomer Frank Drake, took place in 1960.

Despite considerable effort by organizations such as SETI (Search for Extraterrestrial Intelligence), no evidence for extraterrestrial radio transmissions has been found. Some people believe there is little chance for success, since the rapid pace of technological change means that it would be unlikely for two different civilizations to find themselves at a similar state of science and technology. A civilization only slightly younger than Earth's may know nothing of radio waves—after all, people on this planet only discovered radio waves in the late 19th century—and a civilization slightly older may be using communication technology that people on Earth have not even thought of yet. But even though there may only be a small chance of finding intelligent life beyond Earth, such a discovery would be so amazing that some people will continue to keep their radio telescopes "listening" to the stars.

Microwaves

Radio waves called microwaves are important to astronomers for a different reason. Microwaves, which have a smaller ("micro") wavelength than the waves commonly used for radio and television, inform astronomers of events occurring at the very beginning of the universe.

But the initial use of microwaves had a more humble origin. Engineer and inventor Percy Spencer noticed in 1945 that a candy bar melted in his pocket when he came close to a magnetron, a device used in radar that produces a large quantity of microwaves. Spencer, an employee of Raytheon Corporation, investigated the effects on various materials such as popcorn kernels—which popped—and an egg, which heated and burst. Spencer had discovered the idea behind the microwave oven.

Microwaves have a higher frequency than that of other radio waves but not nearly as high as that of visible light, so microwaves do not have much energy per wave. Microwaves do not cook food because of their energy; they cook food because they are at the right frequency to shake up water molecules (H_2O). Water molecules are a common component of food and are polar—the oxygen atom of a water molecule pulls at the negatively charged electrons more strongly than the hydrogen atoms, giving the oxygen atom a small negative charge and the hydrogen atoms small positive charges. (See figure on page 105.) These electrical poles mean that water molecules respond to electric and magnetic fields, such as a passing electromagnetic wave—a microwave.

A microwave oven generates radiation at a frequency of about 2.45 *gigahertz* (billion hertz), a frequency that penetrates deeply into food but does not pass right through it. The rapidly alternating fields of radiation align the water molecules first in one direction, then the other, as shown on page 105. Nearly two and a half billion times per second the water molecules turn back and forth, colliding and generating heat. This process heats the food evenly from center to surface.

Objects like plastic or ceramic plates are not as affected since they contain little water. (Dishes or cups holding food or liquid do get hot because heat travels from the food or liquid into the container.) Metal reflects microwaves, and the oven itself is made of metal to confine the radiation. The door of the oven also reflects microwaves and keeps the energy inside, even though the metal door contains holes. The wavelength of the radiation is much larger than the hole diameter, so microwaves bounce off instead of passing through or scattering, just as radio waves or light waves

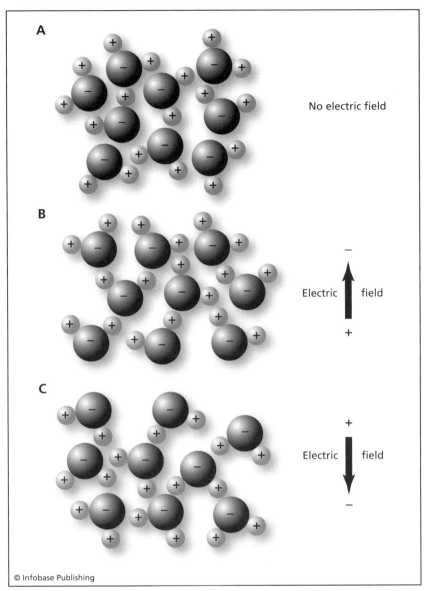

A

No electric field

B

Electric field

C

Electric field

© Infobase Publishing

Water molecules have a small positive charge at the two hydrogen atoms (small circles) and a small negative charge at the oxygen atom (large circle). In the absence of an electric field, as in (a), water molecules are randomly oriented. When an electric field is present, water molecules become oriented, with the negative charge attracted to the positive end of the field, as in (b) and (c). When the electric field oscillates like an electromagnetic wave, the water molecules turn back and forth rapidly.

reflect from a surface or mirror as long its bumps or holes, if any, are smaller than the wavelength. Though the holes in a microwave oven's door are too small for microwaves, visible light, with its smaller wavelength, passes through, which is why the holes are present: to let a person see inside.

Arno Penzias and Robert Wilson made a discovery in 1965 that got astronomers extremely interested in microwaves. Like Karl Jansky, Penzias and Wilson were searching for the source of unwanted noise; they found that at certain frequencies the noise came from all directions in space. This noise proved to be the remnant of the explosion that created the universe, which, as discussed in chapter 1, is expanding. Astronomers believe this cosmic microwave background radiation is similar to an afterglow caused by the tremendous heat and energy released at the moment of creation, the "big bang." Penzias and Wilson received the 1978 Nobel Prize in physics for their discovery.

Scientists study the cosmic microwave background radiation to gather clues of the universe's history, which in turn leads to a better understanding of its present shape. In 2001, NASA launched a space probe, the *Wilkinson Microwave Anisotropy Probe* (*WMAP*), to provide sensitive measurements from every direction in space. The big bang occurred about 14 billion years ago and the temperature of the radiation remnant is frigid, close to −454.7°F (−270.4°C), only about 2.73 degrees above *absolute zero,* the coldest possible temperature. *WMAP* makes an image of the radiation by measuring the difference in temperature of opposite directions (the existence of such differences is called anisotropy). Astronomers use these measurements to determine the age of the universe as well as its geometry. *WMAP* indicates that the universe has a flat rather than a curved geometry.

Infrared and Ultraviolet

Electromagnetic radiation with a slightly higher frequency (and therefore a slightly shorter wavelength) than microwaves is in the infrared range. Chapter 5 discussed the many roles in biology and medicine played by infrared radiation, and all objects whose temperature is at or around the same temperature as the human body emit large amounts of infrared. But the study of infrared also offers much to interest astronomers.

The discoverer of infrared was British astronomer Sir William Herschel (1738–1822). One day in 1800 Herschel spread sunlight into its spectrum, as Sir Isaac Newton had done nearly a century and a half earlier. What interested Herschel was the temperature of the different colors, so he placed a thermometer among each of the colored lights and noted that these thermometers showed a temperature higher than that shown by a nearby shaded thermometer. Then Herschel put a thermometer beneath the red end of the spectrum—in an area where there was no visible light—and was astonished to discover that the temperature of this region was also high. As noted in chapter 5, this radiation became known as infrared, which means "beneath red."

Astronomers study infrared to learn more about objects in space that are not hot enough to emit much visible light, such as small and dim stars, extrasolar planets, and large clouds of dust and gas. Like warm objects on Earth, these bodies do not shine but they do give off a lot of infrared, which can be detected by instruments similar to the telescopes discussed in chapter 2.

Some wavelengths of infrared pass through the dust and gas of Earth's atmosphere but some do not. To study the wavelengths that fail to penetrate the atmosphere, astronomers resort to telescopes orbiting in space. The largest infrared space telescope is NASA's *Spitzer Space Telescope,* launched in August 2003. Orbiting the Sun at about the same distance as Earth (but at a different spot in the orbit, in order to avoid the planet's infrared emissions), the *Spitzer Space Telescope* uses its 33.5-inch (0.85-m) telescope to detect infrared with wavelengths of 0.000118–0.0071 inches (0.0003–0.018 cm). Because all warm objects emit infrared, including a telescope, *Spitzer*'s instruments must be cooled to frigid temperatures so that they do not interfere with the observations. On board the craft are 95 gallons (360 l) of liquid helium to keep the temperature within a few degrees of absolute zero.

Astronomers using *Spitzer* have already made many discoveries. In 2005, for instance, Lin Yan, of the Spitzer Science Center at the

SPACE INFRARED TELESCOPE FACILITY

The *Spitzer Space Telescope* (formerly the *Space Infrared Telescope Facility [SIRTF]*), shown here in five different views, performs observations in the infrared portion of the electromagnetic spectrum. *(NASA/JPL-Caltech)*

California Institute of Technology, found organic (carbon-containing) compounds called polycyclic aromatic hydrocarbons in galaxies at a distance of about 10 billion *light-years* (a light year is the distance light travels in a year). These compounds are important building blocks of life on Earth, and Yan's discovery marks the first time such molecules have been found at such a great distance.

NASA plans to launch a much larger telescope called the *James Webb Space Telescope* in 2013. This telescope will also concentrate on infrared wavelengths and will undoubtedly make new and exciting discoveries.

Another type of invisible electromagnetic radiation is ultraviolet, located on the other side of visible light in the spectrum. The discovery of ultraviolet radiation followed soon after that of infrared; its discoverer, German physicist Johann Ritter (1776–1810), had heard of Herschel's work. Ritter was curious to see if invisible radiation existed beyond the blue or violet end of the light spectrum, so he set up an experiment with silver chloride, which turns dark when exposed to light. After spreading sunlight into its spectrum, Ritter placed silver chloride in a region well beyond (ultra-) the violet light and was delighted to see the compound darken.

Ultraviolet's higher frequency and shorter wavelength mean it is an energetic form of electromagnetic radiation. The range of ultraviolet extends from just beyond visible light—this radiation is known as near ultraviolet, because it is near visible light—to the high end of its spectrum, called extreme ultraviolet, in which the frequency is only slightly less than that of X-rays.

The Sun emits a lot of ultraviolet. Bright new stars in the galaxy emit even larger quantities of ultraviolet, and astronomers study the activity and evolution of these objects by monitoring these frequencies. But since the Earth's atmosphere blocks most of these frequencies, astronomers must use space telescopes like *Hubble*, which works well with ultraviolet radiation, in order to make their observations.

Atmospheric blocking of ultraviolet annoys astronomers but has its advantages. Ultraviolet radiation in large doses has enough energy to damage the cells and tissues of the body, often by breaking down important molecules such as DNA. As mentioned in chapter 1, the atmosphere's ozone layer, consisting of molecules of ozone (three oxygen atoms combined), absorbs much of the Sun's ultraviolet radiation, but a small amount manages to pass through to the surface. On a summer day, when the Sun is overhead and the maximum amount of ultraviolet radiation seeps through the atmosphere, lengthy exposure causes the skin to get sunburned. As a defense against ultraviolet damage, the skin has a dark molecule called melanin that absorbs ultraviolet radiation; repeated exposure to sunlight increases the melanin and the skin darkens. But for all people, light- and dark-skinned alike, too much ultraviolet radiation is unhealthy.

X-rays and Gamma Rays

X-rays and gamma rays are electromagnetic radiation with an extremely high frequency. Gamma rays, the highest-frequency radiation, have so much energy that they are quite dangerous to humans. Yet this radiation, along with X-rays, also has plenty of important applications in medicine as well as in astronomy.

German physicist Wilhelm Röntgen (1845–1923) accidentally discovered X-rays in 1895 when he was experimenting with electric discharges in a device called a vacuum tube, which is a small container from which most of the air has been pumped out. The vacuum tube emitted some sort of radiation that Röntgen noticed was able to excite a phosphor-coated screen. He denoted the radiation with the letter X to specify its unknown nature—at the time of the discovery no one knew that these rays were high-frequency electromagnetic radiation—and the name stuck.

X-ray photons are so energetic that many of them pass right by small atoms such as carbon, oxygen, nitrogen, and hydrogen. Skin and most other body tissue consist mostly of these atoms, so these body parts do not absorb many X-ray photons. But bones contain a considerable number of heavier atoms such as calcium and phosphorus that absorb X-ray photons more frequently. As a result, bones create "shadows" on a film designed to show X-rays—the radiation passes through soft tissue of the body but not the bones, so physicians can take an image of bones without making an incision in the patient. (Most tissue also has subtle differences in absorption that can be detected by x-raying, though such images are not as clear.) To yield even more information, a process called computed tomography (CT) takes X-rays from different positions and angles and converts these individual pictures into a three-dimensional image of the patient.

Gamma rays made their first appearance in science just a few years after X-rays. French physicist Paul Villard (1860–1934) was working with uranium in 1900 when he observed a previously unknown high-energy radiation. A few years later British/New Zealand physicist Ernest Rutherford (1871–1937) showed that these rays were electromagnetic radiation and called them gamma rays, a third type of radiation associated with radioactive material. (Alpha and beta, the first two letters of the Greek alphabet, were the names of the first two types, and gamma is the third letter of the Greek alphabet.)

A single X-ray or gamma-ray photon has enough energy to break chemical bonds that hold together compounds and knock out electrons of atoms or molecules, creating ions—charged molecules. This kind of damage will kill cells and destroy tissue, making ionizing radiation such as X-rays and especially gamma rays dangerous. Medical X-ray machines do not emit enough photons to cause a lot of damage, but some machines used in the treatment of cancer purposely do so. These machines, involved in radiation therapy, kill cancerous cells by subjecting them to large amounts of high-energy X-rays or gamma rays.

X-ray machines create radiation by smashing electrons into atoms, but there are a number of different processes that create X-rays and gamma rays, and many of them exist throughout the universe. Fortunately, Earth's atmosphere protects people on the surface by absorbing most of this radiation before it reaches the ground, which means that astronomers who wish to study X-ray and gamma-ray sources must turn to observatories in space.

Observatories for X-rays or gamma rays are quite different than are those made to observe other forms of electromagnetic waves. Telescopes such as radio telescopes described in this chapter as well as the optical telescopes described in chapter 2 are not possible, since high-energy radiation would burrow into mirrors or pass through lenses with little effect. One of the most important observatories for X-rays is NASA's *Chandra X-ray Observatory*, an orbiting spacecraft launched in July, 1999. *Chandra*'s instruments guide the X-ray photons into a detector by sending them through a barrel-shaped guide. The X-ray photons graze the highly polished inner surface and ricochet off into the detector. Gamma rays also pose serious problems, and observatories usually detect these energetic photons by their interactions with matter—for instance, certain crystals will emit a flash of light when they absorb a gamma-ray photon.

Chandra and similar spacecraft observatories report on some of the most energetic events in the universe. Colliding galaxies, exploding stars, and other enormously violent phenomena release enough energy to generate a huge quantity of X-ray and gamma-ray photons. But large-scale events are not the only sources of high-frequency radiation. Small particles that are accelerated to tremendous velocities can also emit such radiation. These particles and their radiation allow astronomers to study objects such as black holes that are otherwise invisible. A black hole is black because it is so dense that not even light can escape—yet these strange objects can be "seen" because their immensely powerful gravitation attracts and accelerates pieces of matter, giving them enough energy to emit high-frequency radiation.

Electromagnetic radiation of all frequencies is useful in astronomy, and in ways that are sometimes not at all obvious. Visible light—which is obvious even to the unaided eye—forms a mere sliver of the electromagnetic spectrum, and the low frequencies of radio on up to the high frequencies of X-rays and gamma rays offer unique opportunities to learn more of the universe's secrets.

7

COMMUNICATING WITH ELECTROMAGNETIC RADIATION

ECEMBER 26, 2004, is a day that will live in the memories of
many people for a long time. On this day a gigantic tsunami,
caused by a massive earthquake under the Indian Ocean, swept
over Indonesia, Sri Lanka, Thailand, southern India, and other
areas, killing about 250,000 people. Even though these places are
far removed from the United States—Indonesia is roughly 8,500
miles (13,600 km) from California—many Americans knew about
the disaster almost the minute it occurred, as images of the devas-
tation showed up on their television sets.

News travels fast. This has not always been true, although in the
19th century Americans thought that the Pony Express was fast.
News from St. Joseph, Missouri, the westernmost point of railroad
tracks and telegraph offices in 1860, could travel the nearly 2,000
miles (3,200 km) to Sacramento, California, in about 10 days on
average, carried by riders who mounted fresh horses at stations
positioned at intervals along the route. The record speed for the
Pony Express to cover the journey was a little more than seven days,
which occurred in March, 1861, and which carried the inaugural
address of President Abraham Lincoln. (Just a few months later

the Pony Express riders hung up their spurs and retired because of the telegraph's completion.) News was even slower by ship across the Atlantic Ocean: In January 8, 1815, American and British soldiers fought the Battle of New Orleans despite the signing of a treaty in Ghent, Belgium, on December 24, 1814, to end the war. News of the treaty had not yet reached the United States.

Today's global communication networks carry news at the speed of light. Chapter 4 discussed communication carried in optical fibers by electromagnetic waves in the infrared range, and chapter 6 included a description of the radio wave portion of the spectrum. This chapter focuses on wireless communication and broadcasting, which spread news, information, and conversation via radio waves. People can stay informed in a timely manner with these methods, avoiding needless conflicts and sending help soon after horrifying disasters such as the 2004 tsunami.

Antennas and Broadcasting

Electrical communication signals can travel along a wire, as in the old telegraph system or the copper wire of today's "landline" telecommunications. These systems are fast but not always convenient, since they only work where wires are strung and maintained. Radio communication can take place anywhere, even when one or both of the participants are in motion, but wireless technology has two requirements: transmission and reception. Both of these requirements start with an antenna.

An antenna is a device that can emit or receive radio waves. Most simple antennas are in the form of a vertical metal bar or rod that conducts electricity, although much more complex arrangements of bars or loops of wire are possible. The process of generating radio waves begins with a back-and-forth motion of electric charges at some frequency—the frequency of the radio wave.

Danish physicist Hans Christian Oersted (1777–1851) discovered in 1820 that electrical charges in motion produce a magnetic field, and British physicist Michael Faraday (1791–1867) found in 1831 that a changing magnetic field induces an electrical current. But as mentioned in chapter 1, until Scottish physicist James Clerk Maxwell (1831–79) came along, no one realized that an electrical charge undergoing acceleration—a change in motion—releases

Maxwell's Equations

Before the work of James Clerk Maxwell, the physics describing forces and motions of electrical charges and magnets consisted of separate laws and principles discovered by such scientists as Hans Christian Oersted, Michael Faraday, Charles-Augustin de Coulomb, André-Marie Ampère, and others. Maxwell decided to concentrate not so much on the charges and magnets themselves but on the space surrounding them—the electric and magnetic fields, concepts introduced by Faraday that Maxwell had learned from reading Faraday's papers. Maxwell was a theoretical physicist—he did his work with pen, paper, and his imagination—and he was a gifted mathematician. Maxwell derived a set of equations in the 1860s that encompassed all the electrical and magnetic interactions of matter. In modern notation, this set consists of four equations that form the basis for all the physics of electromagnetism.

Maxwell's equations involve advanced mathematics and will not be reproduced here. Despite their complexity, the equations offer a compact and elegant formulation of electromagnetism, a large and varied branch of physics. To Maxwell's brilliant mind, the equations did even more; he noticed that the equations predicted the existence of propagating electric and magnetic fields. This was a new and strange idea, since most physicists had previously spent little time thinking about such abstract notions and had instead focused on more substantial objects such as charges and magnets. But Maxwell linked this new idea to something much more familiar when he realized that the equations predicted the speed of these propagating fields to be the same as that of light. Maxwell inferred that light consists of propagating electric and magnetic fields—light is an electromagnetic wave.

Maxwell's theories needed to be tested and verified, and German physicist Heinrich Hertz (1857–94) performed a series of simple experiments in the 1880s. Maxwell said that charges experiencing a change in motion will produce electromagnetic waves, so Hertz constructed a primitive transmitter consisting of a circuit with oscillating charges and a spark gap. To detect the electromagnetic waves, Hertz built a receiver made of a loop of wire with a small gap. When the transmitter was turned on, the oscillating charges produced sparks, and the receiver—placed a short distance away—also began sparking, which meant that some sort of electromagnetic radiation had traveled across the intervening space and generated oscillating charges in the receiver's circuit. The speed of this radiation was the same as light, proving the existence of electromagnetic waves with the properties predicted by Maxwell.

energy in the form of changing electric and magnetic fields that propagate through space. These propagating electric and magnetic fields are the electromagnetic waves of light, radio, and all other frequencies of the spectrum. As discussed in the sidebar on page 115, Maxwell got his inspiration from a set of equations he formulated to describe the physics of electromagnetism.

An alternating current flowing through an antenna sets the charges oscillating and they emit electromagnetic radiation in all directions (although some antennas tend to emit more radiation in a specific direction). After Heinrich Hertz discovered radio waves in the 1880s, people quickly realized these waves could be used to send signals. But there were several problems. One of the main problems involved the way that radio waves travel—in a straight line.

Flying straight and true is a desirable feature of an arrow but not necessarily of a medium of communication. Sound tends to spread out so that people do not have to face each other in order to talk, but electromagnetic waves are different—once light or radio waves start a journey, they tend to keep on course. This means that if a person wants to communicate with an audience using electromagnetic waves, the audience's receiver should be in the line of sight of the transmitter. Reception is otherwise shaky and unreliable.

The line-of-sight requirement means that if a transmitter is to reach a wide audience, it must be tall. A person standing on top of a skyscraper gets a magnificent view of the surroundings, and this is exactly what a transmitter needs—to have its audience "in sight." Radio waves can pass through thin walls and windows, so the receiver's antenna can be located indoors; stones and other material block the transmission, so the best reception occurs when the antenna is outside.

Broadcasters such as radio and television stations want to reach the largest possible audience, so the stations broadly cast their transmissions from towers specially built for the purpose or (particularly in large cities) make use of the tall buildings already in place. The tallest building in New York City for many years was the 1,250-foot (381-m) Empire State Building, finished in 1931.

Rooftops of skyscrapers offer breathtaking views as well as being excellent locations for broadcaster's antennas. This building is in Philadelphia. *(Kyle Kirkland)*

In 1950 a construction crew installed a 222-foot (68-m) antenna tower on top of the building, and most of the radio and television stations in the city used it. When the World Trade Center towers appeared in the early 1970s, broadcasters switched to these taller buildings—only to switch back after the tragedy of September 11, 2001, when both of the World Trade Center towers were destroyed.

Height is useless if the antenna does not radiate enough energy to reach the ground. Antennas are complex and many factors such as their length and structure are important for proper operation, but one basic requirement is that they be big enough to carry a lot of current. Broadcasting a signal to widespread areas requires a large amount of radiation, and this means a large amount of current flowing in the antenna. If the antenna's conductor is too small, then the heat generated by the current will damage it. The power rating of an antenna specifies the maximum allowable power, which in electrical terms means voltage multiplied by current. The unit of power used in antenna ratings is usually the watt, the same unit that electric utility companies use to compute their customers' bills. More watts mean more power to reach a wider audience. For example, KYW, a news radio station in Philadelphia, transmits with a powerful 50,000 watts.

The first person to transmit and receive radio waves, Heinrich Hertz, produced a humble amount of radiation that barely traveled a few feet. Hertz noticed the difficulties of using radio waves for communication, including a problem that he felt would be hard to solve: When two or more transmitters operate in the same space, a receiver picks up both of the transmissions. This is a problem because the transmissions interfere and any message will be garbled.

Radio and Television

Allowing only one transmitter per city would mean only one available channel of communication—one radio station or one television channel and nothing else. Deciding who would get to use the channel would cause a lot of conflict in a big city like Los Angeles or New York City. But fortunately for people who like variety, there is another solution. Multiple antennas can transmit in the same area and use the same "airwaves" if they broadcast with different frequencies. One of the first stations to broadcast in the United States was KDKA in Pittsburgh on November 2, 1920.

Deciding who gets to use which frequencies could have been another thorny issue, but in the United States this decision is made for most applications by a government agency called the *Federal Communications Commission* (FCC). Established in 1934, the FCC regulates communications by radio and television in all 50 states, the District of Columbia, and U.S. territories. This agency divides the electromagnetic spectrum from 9,000 to 275,000,000,000 hertz into bands that are to be used only for certain purposes. For example, the frequency range between 5,450,000 and 5,680,000 hertz is one of the many bands reserved for aviation communication, and the frequency range between 88,000,000 and 108,000,000 hertz is for FM (*frequency modulation*) radio broadcasting.

Bands for broadcasters become further divided, with each broadcaster getting its own frequency. Nobody can use the same broadcast frequency in the same area, although if the antennas are far apart stations can use overlapping frequencies with little threat of interference.

To receive the broadcasts, the audience needs an antenna in which the electromagnetic waves induce a current—reversing the transmission process—and electronic circuitry to recover the message. The main frequency of a broadcast is called its carrier frequency because it carries the message. The message is composed of variations of some sort, such as changes in amplitude of the signal or small changes in the frequency. Any kind of communication uses such variations; for example, books contain many different words and symbols arranged in a certain order. An unvarying tone of 100,000 hertz would communicate little information, so broadcasts vary—modulate—the signal to incorporate the message. AM (*amplitude modulation*) radio stations vary the amplitude, and FM stations vary the frequency, though not so much that the transmissions interfere with other stations.

Picking out the right frequency is the job of the tuner. Broadcasts from many different stations strike an antenna and induce currents of many different frequencies, one for each station. The tuner consists of a circuit that allows the passage of only a small range of frequencies, and only one station's broadcast gets through. Tuners work because they resonate at certain frequencies, meaning that when signals of the right frequency travel through them the signals grow stronger, while other frequencies become weak and vanish. Changing the resonant frequency of a radio tuner usually means adjusting circuit components called capacitors or other components called inductors. The channel selector on a radio or television does this as the listener switches stations.

Increasing the height of the receiving antenna is a good strategy for the same reason as it is for transmitters—more stations can be "seen." People usually mount their television antenna on top of their roof, gaining as much altitude as possible. These antennas are often the Yagi-Uda type, designed to operate in the range of frequencies used by television broadcasters. One of the rods of the antenna acts to pick up the signals, and the other rods increase the

A Yagi-Uda antenna, shown here on a house in Philadelphia, is sometimes called a "television aerial." *(Kyle Kirkland)*

amount of signal of the desired frequency range by directing or reflecting the radiation. These antennas capture more of the right frequencies and less of the other frequencies (which are always present), making the tuner's job a little easier.

High altitude is essential but clearly there is only so far an antenna can go. Sometimes radio wave signals in the AM band can be heard for long distances at night because a layer in the atmosphere called the ionosphere reflects AM frequencies. (The ionosphere gets its name from the presence of charged particles called ions.) This layer moves higher at night, letting AM signals soar into the sky and then bounce back down, sometimes repeatedly over a wide area. Listeners can occasionally tune into an AM station from another area, sometimes one that is quite far away. Some AM stations have to reduce their transmitting power at night to prevent interference with other, distant stations.

But long-distance reception is rare, unless the signals travel along wires or cables for part of the route, as with cable television. Earth is a sphere, and except for occasional reflections, radio waves do not follow the curved surface of the planet. Television transmission across the Atlantic Ocean, for instance, was impossible until people were able to put transmitters in space.

Satellites orbit Earth at various altitudes, hundreds or even thousands of miles in space. To stay aloft, a satellite must be moving quickly and at a precise speed—too slow and the satellite drops to the ground, too fast and it flies off into space. The appropriate speed depends on the satellite's altitude, and at each possible altitude, any orbiting satellite revolves around the planet at a precise rate. At one particular altitude—22,200 miles (35,500 km) above the surface—satellites revolve around the Earth once each 24 hours. Satellites in this orbit match the rotation rate of the Earth, so to a person on the ground the satellites do not seem to move—they are stationary in the sky. In this orbit, which is called a geosynchronous or geostationary orbit, satellites can behave like tremendously tall antennas, broadcasting to an area covering a vast portion of the planet.

News networks and people who need instant communication all over the globe rely on satellite communication.

Many people now receive television signals with a satellite dish. *(Kyle Kirkland)*

Satellite-based television and radio have also appeared, and on many houses across the United States the Yagi-Uda rooftop antenna has been replaced or supplemented by a satellite dish. These dishes capture signals from satellite transmissions, which are often in the microwave range; for best reception, the dish should be properly oriented to point in the direction where the satellite is located.

Wireless communication is not limited to broadcasters. Radios such as Citizens Band (CB) radios, often used by truck drivers, and police radios transmit and receive information via radio waves. But in the last 15 years radio waves have become an even more popular means of personal communication. Electromagnetic waves carry millions of person-to-person conversations every day conducted by the millions of people who use cell phones.

Cell Phones

Old-fashioned landline telephones work by turning sound waves into electrical signals and transmitting them over copper wires or, more often these days, by turning sound waves into light signals and transmitting them via fiber optics. But being within reach of a wire or cable does not suit many people in today's mobile society. Cell phones, also known as mobile phones, have been around since the 1940s, developed by engineers working at the research facility of the major phone company of the time, Bell Labs. But early mobile phones were bulky, expensive, and limited. Mobile phones did not become popular until the late 1980s and early 1990s, when the phones became smaller and faster and communication companies began to invest money in the networks and technology to connect them. The connection was not by wire but by radio wave.

A cell phone is a radio that uses two frequencies. This is important because radios such as walkie-talkies use a single frequency, so only one person can transmit at a time. With single-frequency radios, people often end their transmission by saying, "Over," because this lets the people they are talking to know it is their turn to transmit. Cell phones use one frequency for sending information and one for receiving, so both transmitter and receiver of a device can work at the same time.

But not everyone can use the same two frequencies. Cell phones emit radiation with only a small amount of power, so they work within a limited region called a cell (hence the term *cell phone*). A cell phone contains a transmitter and antenna, and communicates with a base or tower within the cell. The towers are tall, either constructed specifically for the purpose or installed on top of tall buildings, and have a much greater power and range than the phone. The area of the cell is usually small, about five to 10 square miles ($12.8-25.6$ km^2); when a caller wishes to talk to someone outside of the cell, the tower communicates with other towers and passes the signals along until they reach their destination, which can be another cell phone or a link to a landline telephone. The companies that provide cell phone service have a number of different frequencies for their use, and they divide these frequencies among their cells so that there is no overlap or interference.

The cell phone system divides the country into a large number of cells, providing excellent coverage in heavily populated areas, where there is always a tower nearby, and much sparser coverage

In August 2005, Hurricane Katrina damaged this cell phone tower in Clinton, Mississippi, leaving residents in the neighborhood with unreliable cell phone service until repairs were made. *(Kyle Kirkland)*

in deserts and other thinly populated areas. As a cell phone user travels from cell to cell, one tower hands off the transmission to the next, similar to the way that air traffic controllers hand over responsibility of keeping track of a jet as it moves from one radar range to another. For cell phones it is the strength of the signal that makes the switch—the equipment of each tower automatically monitors all signals close to its area, taking over responsibility of signals that are increasing in strength as the phone user moves into its cell.

But each cell phone company has limited means, and none of them can afford to have towers that span the whole globe. Sometimes cell phone users suffer the annoyance of a conversation that goes out of the range of all towers and gets "dropped." At other times the call may have to get picked up by the tower of another service provider—this is called "roaming"—in which case the cell phone user may find extra charges on his or her bill.

The expense of constructing and maintaining cell phone towers has led at least one state in the United States to consider an alternative. North Dakota has a lot of land and not many people, so there are not enough customers to justify the expense of a huge number of towers. A possible solution is to use balloons drifting at altitudes of 10 to 20 miles (16–32 km). The balloons are cheaper than a tower and with this kind of altitude, a small number could provide coverage for the whole state at a fraction of the cost incurred by an adequate number of towers. Testing of this idea is set to begin in the next few years.

Whether this idea works or not, the principles are valid. Communication over long distances with radio waves requires an antenna with a lot of power and a great deal of altitude. This sophisticated means of communication is certainly faster than the old Pony Express or even telegraphs, but that does not necessarily mean that no simple, old-fashioned solutions exist to the problems of radio communication. Satellites and wireless networks connect the world with instant communication, but radio waves remain as they were when Heinrich Hertz hooked up his primitive transmitter.

8

EXPANDING THE VISUAL HORIZON

A SMALL PLANE flying at an altitude of 30,000 feet (9,150 m) does not cast a visible shadow even during the daylight hours—it does not block enough sunlight—and is difficult to see from the ground. Yet planes loaded with bombs can make their presence felt by unleashing devastating explosions capable of leveling a city. Although the early planes of the 20th century were not able to do much damage, by the 1940s, during World War II, fleets of bombers had become deadly weapons. Bombing raids caused much destruction and loss of life.

To defend their factories, as well as their cities and citizens, nations had to develop methods of expanding their vision. As discussed in chapters 2 and 6, telescopes are effective at gathering and observing light or other wavelengths of electromagnetic radiation emitted by distant objects, but these instruments were of little use in spotting bombers because the enemy planes kept as dark as possible. In order to see the incoming planes the defenders had to supply the light—or other wavelengths of electromagnetic radiation—for illumination.

The job of finding and targeting the rapidly moving airplanes is not as simple as shining a flashlight to light up a cellar on a dark night. The bombers may be flying four to five miles (6.4–8.0

km) high, and to get an early warning of a raid the defenders need to detect the planes from miles away, long before they fly overhead. Locating an object at these great distances required new developments in the physics and technological applications of electromagnetic waves.

Searching with Light

American inventor Thomas Edison (1847–1931) developed the electric lightbulb in 1879, and although this invention brought about cheap and effective illumination, the filaments in these bulbs were not exceptionally bright. Theater companies around this time would light their stages with intense beams produced by putting lime (calcium oxide) in a flame generated by burning oxygen and hydrogen gases. (This is the origin of the term *limelight,* meaning a spotlight of attention.) It was not until 1918, late in World War I, that American engineer Elmer Sperry (1860–1930) developed a remarkably powerful searchlight.

The war did much to motivate Sperry's invention, because military planners wanted to increase their night attacks as well as to spot enemy airplanes. Sperry's searchlight made its light from two rods of carbon connected to a source of electrical current. When the rods touch and then separate, forming a small gap between them, the electrical charges jump the short distance and the temperature of the carbon tips rises to about 3,000°F (1,650°C). The heat causes the carbon tips to glow with an intensely bright light. In Sperry's searchlights the beam had the power of about 800 million candles and could illuminate objects five to six miles (8.0–9.6 km) away. These searchlights are called carbon arc lights.

But producing the light is only part of the solution. To light up a distant target, a searchlight must focus its light in a tight, narrow beam, rather than throwing the radiation out in all directions. The problem is that light generated by heating—incandescent light—spreads out, unlike the coherent light of lasers (described in chapter 4). The job of focusing the carbon arc's intense light was done by a curved mirror, the same sort of device that telescopes use.

The figure on page 24 of chapter 2 illustrates how a concave mirror focuses light onto a single point, the focal point. In a reflecting telescope, the parallel rays of light coming from a distant light source strike the mirror and bounce to the focal point (that is, if the mirror is properly curved in a paraboloid shape, or at least close to a paraboloid; a spherical shape fails to focus perfectly but will often work well enough). Sperry's searchlight works similarly, although in reverse. Many of the rays from a source of light positioned in a concave mirror's focal point will get directed outward into a parallel beam—imagine the lines in part (a) on page 24 in the same position but going the opposite direction. Some of the light will be lost but if the light is strong enough, an intense beam results.

In the early years of World War II, the German Luftwaffe (Air Force) launched many bombing raids on England in the attempt to force surrender. The British fought back by installing a large number of searchlights at various locations throughout a chosen line of defense. A group of searchlights fixed their beams on a plane, tracking its movement across the sky, and as the plane moved away and out of range of these searchlights, another group would take up the target. This kept the German bomber illuminated throughout its flight and allowed British antiaircraft gunners to take aim and fire. Later in the war, when the British bombers raided Germany at night, the German defenders adopted similar strategies, dividing the sky into zones that were the responsibility of a number of carefully positioned searchlights.

Other uses for intense sources of light have been required ever since people began sailing the seas. Light beams can carry signals from one ship to another, and at night lighthouses warn sailors of the presence of land, particularly dangerous, rocky coastlines. Lighthouses generate light not to illuminate a distant object but instead to be seen by a ship's captain, who can then prevent the vessel from ramming the rocks and sinking. Before the age of electricity, lighthouses used kerosene or oil lamps and directed the light with the help of silvered reflectors. Then incandescent lamps came into use.

A sailor aboard the USS *Blue Ridge* uses light to send a signal to another ship. *(United States Navy/Photographer's Mate 3rd Class Tucker M. Yates)*

Another method of projecting a lighthouse beam came into use in the 19th century. This method employed a gigantic lens to help gather the light, an idea originated by French physicist Augustin-Jean Fresnel (1788–1827), and called a Fresnel lens in his honor. A Fresnel lens is more complicated than the lenses described in chapter 2 and consists of a series of rings of prisms, positioned concentrically, like the rings of a tree, and at varying angles. These rings bend the rays into a tight group. The biggest lenses were 12 feet (3.6 m) tall, 6 feet (1.8 m) wide, and weighed about 6,000 pounds. With the aid of Fresnel lenses, a lighthouse could send out incandescent light that could be seen for 20 miles (32 km), all the way to the horizon. The rotating or flashing light gave ship captains plenty of warning.

Fresnel lenses have been replaced by searchlight beacons in many lighthouses today, and lighthouses themselves are less important now that sailors have satellite navigation and other tools to chart their course. But simple Fresnel lenses still find employment in projectors and traffic lights. Carbon arc searchlights have also found other jobs, such as performing light shows, but many applications today use xenon arcs that produce light in tubes filled with xenon ions.

While Sperry's searchlights were successful at pinpointing enemy bombers in the night sky, they did not have sufficient range to give the defenders an advance warning of the bombers' arrival. This essential task fell to an electromagnetic wave of a different wavelength than light.

This lighthouse is at Peggy's Cove, on the eastern Canadian shore at Nova Scotia. *(Elizabeth Kirkland)*

Finding Objects and Catching Speeders with Radar

A searchlight emits a bright beam of light that reflects from distant objects, making these objects visible. Sending a powerful beam of radio waves and detecting the "echo" as the waves bounce off objects would work just as well. This is the basis for radar; the name stands for *r*adio *d*etection *a*nd *r*anging. People realized in the early 20th century that radar "vision" was possible, but development waited until the 1930s, when the threat of military air strikes became clear. Researchers working in the United Kingdom, Germany, Japan, the United States, and several other countries secretly designed and constructed their own radar equipment.

Radar works by emitting high-intensity radio waves and searching for and receiving any reflections—radio waves that get bounced back because they reflect from the surface of distance objects. The location of the object is easy to determine by calculating the time elapsed between the emission of the wave and the detection of a reflection; multiplying the elapsed time by the speed of radio waves gives the total distance the wave traveled, and half this distance is the location of the object that reflected the waves. (Halving the distance is necessary because the radio waves make the trip twice—once to the object and then back again to the detector.)

By using radar, countries obtained early warning of approaching airplanes. Radar equipment would emit radio waves in all directions, and when the sensors picked up a reflection coming from a specific direction, the radar operator would concentrate on this area. By moving the radar antenna back and forth, noting which angle had the strongest reflection, operators could determine the direction more precisely.

Although radar indicates the direction and distance of enemy planes, the resolution of early radar equipment was too poor to guide weapons—radar could not locate the planes with enough precision, so gunners had to use their eyes, and at night searchlights were necessary to pick out the targets. But this changed as radar equipment improved. As mentioned in chapter 2, the ability of electromagnetic radiation to "see" details gets better as the wavelength of the waves decreases (or, in other words, as the frequency increases). The key to improving radar's resolution was to use higher-frequency radio waves, and the key to doing that was finding a way to generate them; while transmitters for radio waves of low frequency were simple to make, higher frequencies proved much tougher. In the early 1940s British researchers invented the cavity magnetron, a device that emits a great deal of energy in the microwave portion of the spectrum. (This is the device that engineer Percy Spencer was investigating when he discovered the cooking power of microwaves, as described in chapter 6.) The high-frequency microwaves improved radar's resolution and provided pinpoint locations.

Radars can reveal an object's location by simply measuring the time of travel, but other properties of the electromagnetic wave yield additional information. One of these properties is polarization (not to be confused with polar molecules, discussed earlier). Polarization is the orientation of the electromagnetic fields of the wave, as discussed in the sidebar on page 133.

Radar sites, such as this one in Guam, monitor the skies. *(United States Air Force/ Tech. Sgt. Shane A. Cuomo)*

Transverse Waves and Polarization

A sound wave consists of waves of varying pressure (compression and rarefaction) that travel in the same direction that the wave propagates. An electromagnetic wave consists of changing electric and magnetic fields, and these fields vary in a direction perpendicular to the direction that the wave propagates, as shown in the figure below. This kind of wave is called a transverse wave. (A sound wave is an example of a longitudinal wave.)

The electric and magnetic fields of an electromagnetic wave are perpendicular to each other, but they can be oriented in any manner with respect to the direction of travel. The electric field may be vertical or horizontal (or any angle) or even spinning

(continued on next page)

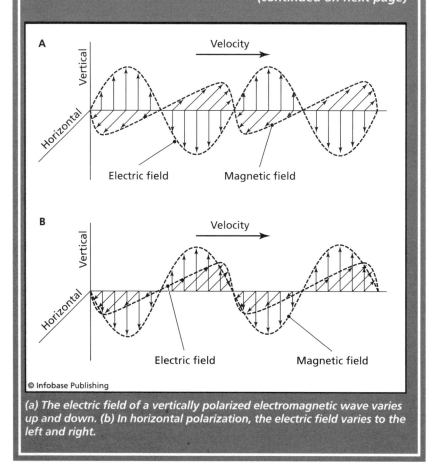

© Infobase Publishing

(a) The electric field of a vertically polarized electromagnetic wave varies up and down. (b) In horizontal polarization, the electric field varies to the left and right.

(continued from previous page)
around and around (in which case the magnetic field will also be spinning around, maintaining a 90-degree angle with the electric field). Many sources of electromagnetic radiation emit waves that do not all have a specific orientation—some of the rays have a vertical electric field and some have a horizontal one. But in some instances the radiation has a dominant orientation, a situation called polarization. Polarized electromagnetic radiation can be vertical, horizontal, or circular (rotating), as given by the orientation of the electric field. (Although the magnetic field orientation would do just as well, people chose the electric field to decide the polarization because most sensors use electric fields to detect electromagnetic radiation.)

Antennas usually emit polarized radiation, oriented in the same direction as the antenna—vertical for vertical antennas and horizontal for horizontal antennas. Reflection can also introduce polarization, because sometimes more waves that are polarized in one direction or another will reflect from a surface. For example, when light strikes a horizontal surface at a shallow angle—as when sunlight reflects from a lake when the Sun is low in the sky—the reflected light contains an abundance of horizontally polarized rays. This is what causes glare. Sunglasses reduce glare because the lenses have a coating of a material that is more transparent to light with vertical polarization than horizontal polarization, which cuts the amount of reflected light to a more tolerable level.

All kinds of objects reflect radiation, so all kinds of objects will be detected by radar. This makes radar useful in many different situations, from locating planes or birds to mapping terrain. Metal objects tend to produce reflections with vertical or horizontal polarization, and rough surfaces like a rocky coastline tend to have nonpolarized reflections. Radar operators who are mapping surfaces with dense vegetation will often use one particular orientation for emission—vertical, perhaps—and then study the perpendicular orientation, which would be horizontal in this case. The reason is that the branches and leaves exist in many orientations and in many layers, and the polarization or change in polarization of the reflection can reveal the type of vegetation and its depth.

Another important property of the reflection is its frequency. As mentioned earlier, resolution depends on frequency, but frequency is important for another reason that is related to the Doppler effect. Chapter 1 of this book includes a sidebar, "The Doppler Effect," explaining this phenomenon, which has many applications throughout physics and optics. The Doppler effect occurs because radiation emitted by or reflected from a moving object changes slightly in frequency; the frequency increases when the object is moving toward an observer and decreases when the object is moving away. Because of the Doppler effect, reflections of a radar's transmission shift in frequency depending on the velocity of the object making the reflection.

There are numerous uses for Doppler radar (equipment designed to detect frequency shifts due to the Doppler effect). Police officers measure the speed of cars on the highway in order to catch those who exceed the limit. Weather forecasters measure the fall of precipitation and its amount and can usually determine which type of precipitation it is, whether rain, snow, or hail. And air traffic controllers use radar to give them a complete picture of all the planes in the sky and how fast and in what direction they are moving.

Although radar is beneficial to people who need to find objects, it is not so beneficial to people who wish to stay hidden. Soon after countries began using radar to warn them of bombing raids, the bombers began to develop the means to "blind" them. A common technique was to drop a huge quantity of metal strips, called chaff, from a plane. These pieces of metal fell slowly or drifted in the wind, and their reflections generated false targets on radar screens.

Another method of countering radar was to emit a large quantity of radiation at the frequencies used by the radar, jamming the radar's receivers and masking the echo reflection. Determining which frequencies to jam was a simple matter of detecting the radar's transmission. Radar must make transmissions of some kind, and if it cannot hear the echo—radiation reflected from a target—it cannot function properly. The detection of strong emissions of radio (including microwave) frequencies is an indication that radar is operating nearby, a process used in the radar detectors bought by drivers who wish to observe the speed limit only when there is a police officer in the vicinity.

The measures to blind radar were naturally countered by radar operators, who relied on multiple pieces of equipment, different frequencies, or strongly polarized radiation. Many police officers are now armed with "lidar"—radar using light instead of microwave frequencies, forcing the radar detector owners to update their equipment. Most of these lidars actually use infrared radiation, not visible light, and they do not measure speed by the Doppler effect. Instead they bounce a laser pulse off the target and measure the elapsed time from transmission to echo, then repeat the process. This gives an indication of speed, because the elapsed time will change from pulse to pulse and the change depends on how fast the object is moving.

But making use of other frequencies will not help if the surface of the target returns hardly any radiation to the radar. This is the goal of stealth technology. Stealth airplanes do not show up well on radar because they scatter or absorb the radar's transmissions. The surfaces of most airplanes are round and smooth because this provides the most efficient aerodynamic shape, reducing air drag. But a stealth airplane is composed of flat surfaces joined with sharp edges, and radar transmissions striking it will reflect in a scattered fashion, most of which is away from the direction of the beam—and therefore away from the radar's receiver, as illustrated in the upper figure on page 137. The surface of a stealth airplane also has a coating of material that tends to absorb electromagnetic radiation rather than reflect it. As a result of the scattering and the absorption, little of the radar's transmission gets reflected back. Although some of the energy returns, the radar detects so little that a stealth plane may look more like a small bird, or its signal may be completely buried in the noise of other reflections.

The first stealth airplane was the F-117A, delivered to the United States Air Force in 1982. The B-2, an Air Force bomber, also uses stealth technology, which among other features boosted its price tag to more than 2 billion dollars—making it one of the

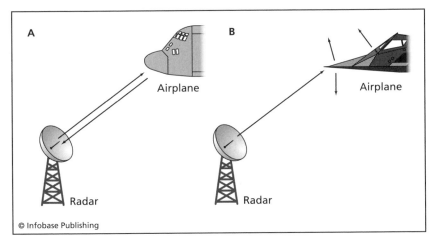

The smooth metal surface of most airplanes reflects radiation back to the radar, as shown in (a). The flat, jointed surfaces of stealth airplanes scatter the radiation (b).

most expensive airplanes ever built. The surfaces, special materials and coatings, and flying-wing shape of the B-2 all make the airplane exceptionally difficult for radar to detect, no matter what frequency of radiation it employs. B-2 aircraft have flown combat missions in Kosovo, Afghanistan, and Iraq.

The B-2 is nearly invisible to enemy radar. *(United States Air Force)*

Seeing through Walls with Terahertz

Stealth airplanes hide from radar by allowing as little radiation to return to the receiver as possible, and people hide objects with a similar though far less expensive strategy—by covering the object with some opaque material such as a newspaper or clothing. Since light does not penetrate the covering, no observer can see the object.

But this simple strategy may soon begin to fail. In the United States, the Department of Homeland Security is interested in developing a device to see through paper, clothing, and other concealing material. The goal is to see concealed weapons such as sharp objects or explosives before an attacker has the opportunity to use them.

Airports and government offices already use metal detectors to screen for weapons, but this technology is not perfect, and nonmetallic weapons such as explosives do not trigger an alarm. Researchers such as John Federici, physics professor at the New Jersey Institute of Technology, are working with a type of electromagnetic radiation called *terahertz* that may do a much better job. Terahertz radiation gets its name from its frequency range—*tera* means "trillion," and terahertz radiation has a frequency in the range of a few trillion hertz, which puts it slightly above microwaves and below infrared on the electromagnetic spectrum. The advantage of terahertz radiation is that it can travel through many materials, such as packaging, bags, walls, clothing, and shoes; to terahertz, these materials are transparent.

Federici and his colleagues want to use terahertz radiation as a probe, somewhat as a physician uses X-rays to probe and image a patient's body. But unlike X-rays, terahertz radiation is not energetic enough to be ionizing (see chapter 6), and there is no risk of injury to a person exposed to this radiation. Terahertz radiation penetrates into concealed spaces and is absorbed or reflected by any metal or chemical explosive that may be hiding there. An analysis of the spectrum of radiation returning to the detector provides clues as to the nature of the hidden objects, giving security personnel a revealing picture unobtainable with visible light.

A lack of powerful emitters of terahertz radiation has delayed the development of terahertz imaging (along with other research and applications of these frequencies), but new devices using gallium arsenide have recently been built and tested. Terahertz instruments will probably soon be used for security screening as well as in hospitals for imaging and medical diagnosis, further expanding the vision of observers who already use radio, microwaves, and other wavelengths of electromagnetic radiation to see in places where visible light fails to reach.

9

ENERGY FROM THE SUN

PLANTS CAPTURE PHOTONS from the Sun to make food and are the foundation on which all life of the planet rests. This process, as described in chapter 5, is the starting point of the food chain. Light propagates the 93.5 million miles (149.6 million km) from Sun to Earth and offers a bountiful supply of an ingredient essential to all forms of motion and life—energy.

The energy in sunlight is obvious in its role of manufacturing food and in its warmth. Cold-blooded animals such as lizards bask in the sunlight to absorb its heat, and even people will turn their faces toward the Sun to warm up on a chilly day in early spring. The power of sunlight to drive motion can be seen in a device created by British scientist Sir William Crookes (1832–1919), consisting of a rotating wheel inside a glass chamber. Vanes attached to the wheel are brightly colored on one side and dark on the other, and when exposed to light the wheel turns. The device is sometimes called a light mill, and although the physics underlying the rotation is not as simple as some people think (and has been the subject of some debate), many science museums display one to illustrate the energy in light.

As a source of energy, sunlight has been relatively neglected until recent times. People have been far more interested in steam, electricity, or petroleum to power their cars and machinery and to heat their homes. But sunlight has advantages that other energy sources cannot possibly achieve, since sunlight is cheap—the Sun makes plenty of it and never sends a bill—and it generates no pollution or hazardous waste. The question today is whether people can make the technology to take full advantage of this tremendous resource.

Capturing the Energy of the Sun

Some instruments have already been made to capture the energy of light. Light-powered calculators never need batteries, and a few signs and emergency call boxes on highways derive their energy from sunlight. These instruments contain components called *photovoltaic cells* to transform the energy of photons into electric current. The term *photovoltaic* derives from the words *photo* (light) and *volt* (electricity), and photovoltaic cells come in many shapes and sizes.

Most photovoltaic cells are made of silicon. In its pure form, this element, the second most abundant in the Earth's crust after oxygen, is a poor conductor of electricity. Pure silicon does not conduct electricity because there are few free and mobile electrons to flow and carry a current, unlike copper and other metals, which have many mobile electrons. But silicon is a semiconductor, and with the addition of a small number of boron or phosphorous atoms, silicon can conduct electricity in one direction in a controlled fashion with the application of a small voltage. Semiconductors made of silicon and other, similar materials are widely used in electronics, where they form the diodes and transistors found in everything from computers to cell phones.

When light strikes a photovoltaic cell, the photons can be absorbed or reflected, or they may pass through. To function efficiently, the cell must absorb as many photons as possible, capturing their energy. When absorbed, the photon's energy frees an electron that is normally stuck, so the electron can move. The electron has a negative charge, and when it moves, the place where it had been attached is now missing a negative charge, so it has a positive charge. These positively charged places are called holes, and other free electrons can move into them. Thus, current flows.

Although photovoltaic cells make electricity from freely available sunlight, the present state of technology is far from ideal. Sunlight's spectrum consists of many different frequencies but only some of these have enough energy to stimulate electricity in silicon photovoltaic cells. As discussed in chapter 1, higher frequencies have more energy, and only high-frequency photons will work in current versions of photovoltaic cells. To make the situation even worse, not all the energy of these high-frequency photons goes into making electricity—creating a free electron and hole requires a specific amount of energy and any excess will be lost, since this energy will not produce electricity in the cell but will instead raise its temperature. Most photovoltaic cells convert only about 10 to 20 percent of light's energy into electricity.

Efficiency concerns are not the only problems with solar energy conversion. Days with clear skies have a lot of sunshine, but nights and cloudy days tend to discourage the use of solar devices. An important step in making photovoltaic cells a practical and reliable technology is the ability either to store electricity for later use or have an alternative supply.

Storing electricity is the job of a battery. Although batteries add to the cost of a solar energy system, they are necessary if energy is needed continually or at various times besides just when the Sun is out. During a sunny day the photovoltaic cells are busy making electricity, which can be used by an appliance or can charge up a battery. At night or on a cloudy day the battery supplies electricity.

The kind of batteries needed by solar energy systems are not cheap and must be replaced every so often. An alternative method of supplying energy in sunless periods is to have another energy input, often from a conventional source such as an electric utility company. In some states of the United States, utility companies allow customers to hook their solar energy systems up to the electricity grid (the network that routes and supplies electricity to a community). Customers pay for the electricity they use but during sunny days, when their solar energy system produces more energy than they need, the utility company buys the excess, which it sells to its other customers.

A single photovoltaic cell's output is usually small, producing only a few watts of power, much less than is required by even a single 60-watt lightbulb. Tying together a number of cells generates more power, enough to at least partly heat a home or provide hot water. But photovoltaic cells and solar energy systems are not yet common in houses and businesses because utility companies generate electricity at a cheaper rate—turning sunlight into electricity costs about five to 15 times as much as using coal or natural gas. Photovoltaic cells work, though not cheaply or efficiently yet.

Solar-Energy-Powered Spacecraft and Probes

Despite the higher expense of transforming solar energy into electricity, under certain circumstances photovoltaic cells prove to be the best option. The power cables of utility companies do not extend beyond the confines of Earth, so orbiting and voyaging spacecraft and probes are on their own when it comes to obtaining power.

Almost all satellites orbiting Earth have some kind of photovoltaic cell to produce the power needed to operate instruments and communication equipment. This includes the *International Space Station,* which has eight arrays containing a total of about 250,000 photovoltaic cells, and the *Hubble Space Telescope,* whose two solar energy panels generate about 2,800 watts of electrical power. These satellites could not function without solar energy. In the manned *International Space Station,* a loss of power could be particularly disastrous.

Ships and probes that escape Earth's gravitational field and venture far into the solar system must also have power, but a difficulty arises if the craft's journey takes it a great distance from the Sun. The distant stars of the night sky appear as only a pinpoint of light, and when a ship or probe is far from the Sun the same situation occurs—only a tiny amount of radiation is available from the Sun. Space probes traveling to outer planets such as Saturn or Neptune usually fill their electricity needs with nuclear energy rather than solar energy. The distance record for photovoltaic cells is held by NASA's *Stardust* probe, which turned the Sun's light into electricity when it was as far away as about 250,000,000 miles (400,000,000 km).

Closer to home is Mars, a planet that is about 142,500,000 miles (228,000,000 km) from the Sun. Mars holds special interest to scientists because it is the most similar to Earth of all the other planets, and at one time in its history water flowed on its surface. To study the geology and chemistry of Mars, NASA has sent rovers to land on the planet and explore its surface. Two of these unmanned probes are the twin rovers *Spirit* (launched June 10, 2003) and *Opportunity* (launched July 7, 2003). Each rover has a panel of photovoltaic cells covering an area of about 14 feet^2 (1.3 m^2). The cells are made from gallium arsenide, stacked in three layers so that they can absorb more of the sunlight falling on the panels. Two lithium batteries provide storage.

Both rovers landed on Mars in January, 2004, and their mission was a spectacular success. The rovers have gathered a huge amount of data—much of which is still being analyzed—and have taken breathtaking pictures. They have also lasted longer in the

This illustration shows one of the twin Mars rovers as it would appear on the surface of the "red planet." *(NASA-JPL)*

harsh conditions than NASA technicians expected. And the rovers continue to move. As of early February, 2006, Spirit had logged four miles (6,430 m) and Opportunity's odometer read slightly more than four miles (6,505 m).

The excellent performance of the Mars rovers offers hope for photovoltaic cells on Earth. Earth, being closer to the Sun than Mars, receives even more solar energy; about 130 watts per square foot (1,400 W/m^2) hits the upper atmosphere of this planet. The atmosphere reflects or absorbs some of the light, but on a clear day when the Sun is high in the sky—which is when the most sunlight is available on the surface, since this is the time when sunlight travels through the least amount of atmosphere to get there—more than half of the energy makes it to the surface. Society has not yet taken advantage of this resource because of the expense associated with transforming it into electricity, but this will change over time. New technologies may cut the cost, and even if this does not happen, solar energy systems, with their lack of pollution and hazardous waste, are in some ways already an improvement over other energy sources.

CONCLUSION

VISION IS ONE of light's greatest gifts to people. From a safe distance, the Sun floods Earth with electromagnetic radiation that ricochets from object to object, and the eyes capture this light, allowing the brain to view the world in all its splendor. The science and technology of optics has yielded even greater vision—including other wavelengths of radiation, such as X-rays and radio waves—along with devices such as the laser to create beams narrow and coherent enough to make the trip to the Moon and back.

The energy of light has not yet been tapped as thoroughly. Plants make food by photosynthesis in a process so important that all life on Earth depends on it, but human technology is less successful at converting light into useful products or forces. Although physicians and metalworkers cut with laser-beam "knives," and photovoltaic cells absorb photons and make electricity, much of the capacity of electromagnetic waves to push, pull, and fuel motion has lain fallow and unused. NASA has tested a small airplane kept aloft by a light beam, as mentioned in chapter 4, and in the coming years light's energy should begin to play a more important role in energy production. It may also give humans their first ride to the stars.

Electromagnetic radiation consists of particles called photons (at least it does when radiation is not behaving as a wave) and photons bounce off and push against other objects as any other particle does. A photon's push is tiny and on the surface of Earth is difficult to detect, since it is lost among a host of more powerful forces. But in the vacuum of space beyond the Earth's atmosphere, the pressure of light acting on an object can have important and noticeable effects. People such as scientist and science fiction writer Robert L. Forward (1932–2002) have proposed a ship for astronauts to sail through the solar system and perhaps even beyond. But instead of wind, light would fill and push these sails. Photons bouncing off a gigantic sail, miles across, could generate enough force to accelerate a ship through space.

Light from the Sun could provide a push as long as the ship was in the vicinity of the solar system (and going in the right direction). For increased maneuverability, and for operation at vast distances from the Sun, Forward suggested training a laser on the sail. A laser's beam does not spread out much with distance and its concentrated energy would be able to push the sail and its passengers or cargo far into the solar system and perhaps beyond. Leik Myrabo, a professor at the Rensselaer Polytechnic Institute, and his colleagues have tested lasers and light sails at special facilities located at White Sands Missile Range, New Mexico. The laser beam lifted the sail ship in one test to an altitude of about 232 feet (71 m).

The short distances in these tests are not discouraging. A light sail encounters strong obstacles of gravity and wind resistance on the surface of the planet, but in space the ship would meet little opposition. With nothing to hold back the ship, a laser could accelerate it to high velocities, and the absence of wind resistance would permit the sail to be thin and fragile yet huge, spanning a large distance and thereby maximizing the number of photons reflected. The low mass, m, of such a sail means a greater acceleration, a, for a given force, F, because Sir Isaac Newton's second law of motion applies: $a = \dfrac{F}{m}$.

To reach tremendous distances of the outer planets of the solar system or to go beyond the solar system, the laser would have to be more powerful than any of the lasers existing today. But in principle such a ship would succeed, and NASA is considering this method of propulsion among others to power future spacecraft. Perhaps one day people may be riding the energy of light all the way to the stars.

SI Units and Conversions

Unit	Quantity	Symbol	Conversion
Base Units			
meter	length	m	1 m = 3.28 feet
kilogram	mass	kg	
second	time	s	
ampere	electric current	A	
Kelvin	thermodynamic temperature	K	1 K = 1°C = 1.8°F
candela	luminous intensity	cd	
mole	amount of substance	mol	
Supplementary Units			
radian	plane angle	rad	π rad = 180 degrees
Derived Units (combinations of base or supplementary units)			
Coulomb	electric charge	C	
cubic meter	volume	m^3	1 m^3 = 1,000 liters = 264 gallons
farad	capacitance	F	
Henry	inductance	H	

Unit	Quantity	Symbol	Conversion
Derived Units (continued)			
Hertz	frequency	Hz	1 Hz = 1 cycle per second
meter/second	speed	m/s	1 m/s = 2.24 miles/hour
Newton	force	N	4.4482 N = 1 pound
Ohm	electric resistance	Ω	
Pascal	pressure	Pa	101,325 Pa = 1 atmosphere
radian/second	angular speed	rad/s	π rad/s = 180 degrees/second
Tesla	magnetic flux density	T	
volt	electromotive force	V	
Watt	power	W	746 W = 1 horsepower

UNIT PREFIXES

Prefixes alter the value of the unit.

Example: kilometer = 10^3 meters (1,000 meters)

Prefix	Multiplier	Symbol
femto	10^{-15}	f
pico	10^{-12}	p
nano	10^{-9}	n
micro	10^{-6}	μ
milli	10^{-3}	m
centi	10^{-2}	c
deci	10^{-1}	d
deca	10	da
hecto	10^2	h
kilo	10^3	k
mega	10^6	M
giga	10^9	G
tera	10^{12}	T

GLOSSARY

absolute zero the lowest possible temperature, -459.67°F (-273.15°C)

adenosine triphosphate a molecule used by most living organisms as an energy source to maintain and support life

AM See AMPLITUDE MODULATION

amplitude the height or intensity of a wave

amplitude modulation the process of conveying information by changing (modulating) the amplitude of a wave

antenna a device, usually metallic, that emits or receives electromagnetic radiation

astigmatism irregularities in the shape of a lens causing a loss of focus

ATP See ADENOSINE TRIPHOSPHATE

bioluminescence the emission of light by living organisms (such as fireflies)

CD See COMPACT DISC

chromatic aberration the focusing defect caused by the tendency of a glass lens to refract different wavelengths (colors) of light by a different amount

coherent light a group of photons (or waves) of light that behave as a single unit and stay close together

compact disc (CD) a device that stores music or computer data in a series of pits or bumps that are read by a laser

concave lens a lens that is thinner in the middle than at the edges, causing rays of light to diverge (spread out)

concave mirror a mirror that curves inward, causing reflected rays of light to converge (move toward each other)

convex lens   a lens that is thicker in the middle than at the edges, causing rays of light to converge (move toward each other)

convex mirror   a mirror that curves outward, causing reflected rays of light to diverge (spread out)

diffraction   a change in the path of a light wave as it moves through an opening or around an obstacle

Doppler effect   a change in the frequency of an emitted wave, as perceived by an observer, when there is relative motion between the source of emission and the observer

DVD   a disc that codes video or computer data in a series of pits or bumps read by a laser

electric field   a region that exerts electrical forces, produced by electromagnetic phenomena

electromagnetic radiation   energy consisting of propagating electric and magnetic fields

electromagnetic wave   See ELECTROMAGNETIC RADIATION

electron   a negatively charged particle and component of an atom, in which it orbits the positively charged nucleus

extrasolar planet   a planet beyond the solar system

FCC   See FEDERAL COMMUNICATIONS COMMISSION

Federal Communications Commission   The United States government agency that regulates radio wave communications

FM   See FREQUENCY MODULATION

focal point   the point at which light rays converge (or appear to diverge from)

frequency   the number of times an event occurs per unit of time; for waves, the number of cycles per unit of time (usually seconds)

frequency modulation   the conveying of information by changing (modulating) the frequency of a wave

gamma rays   electromagnetic radiation with a frequency beyond 5×1019 hertz

gigahertz   a billion hertz

hertz   a unit of frequency equal to one cycle per second

holography   the process of making a three-dimensional image of a scene or an object by recording interference patterns from reflected radiation

hyperopia   farsightedness, the condition in which the eye tends to focus objects behind the retina, resulting in blurry vision for all except distant objects

incandescent light   radiation produced by hot, glowing objects

index of refraction   for a given material, the speed of light in a vacuum divided by the speed of light through that material

infrared   invisible electromagnetic radiation with a frequency slightly lower than red light; the frequency range is roughly 300 billion hertz to 430 trillion hertz

interference   the combining of two or more electromagnetic waves that occupy the same space at the same time, resulting in the distortion of the waves or the reduction of their amplitude to zero

interferometry   measurements, often of distance, based on the interference of electromagnetic waves

laser   light amplification by stimulated emission of radiation, producing bright, intense beams of coherent light

laser-assisted in situ keratomileusis (LASIK)   shaping the cornea with a laser beam to help correct vision problems

LASIK   See LASER-ASSISTED IN SITU KERATOMILEUSIS

lens   a transparent, carefully shaped object that refracts light

light-year   the distance that light travels in one year in a vacuum, equal to about 5,880,000,000,000 miles (9,400,000,000,000 km)

magnetic field   a region that exerts magnetic forces, produced by electromagnetic phenomena

microwaves   electromagnetic waves with a frequency ranging from 1 to 300 billion hertz

mirage   refraction by the atmosphere that causes images of objects to be seen, sometimes in an inverted or magnified form, in places where the objects are not really located

mirror   a smooth, polished surface that reflects light and can form an image

monochromatic   having the light of a single wavelength; if the frequency is in the visible range, it is perceived as a single color

myopia   nearsightedness, the condition in which the eye tends to focus objects in front of the retina, resulting in blurry vision for all except nearby objects

NASA See NATIONAL AERONAUTICS AND SPACE ADMINISTRATION

National Aeronautics and Space Administration The United States government agency responsible for space exploration and technology

normal an imaginary line perpendicular (at a 90-degree angle) to the surface of a lens

nucleus, atomic the positively charged central region of an atom, containing most of its mass

parallax the apparent movement of an object in the field of vision when viewed from a different angle

photon particle of electromagnetic radiation

photoreceptor cell in the retina that responds to light

photovoltaic cell a device capable of absorbing electromagnetic radiation and using the energy to generate electricity

polarization an orientation of the oscillating fields of an electromagnetic wave, such as vertical polarization, when the electric field of the wave is vertical, or horizontal polarization, when the electric field is horizontal

primary colors a small number of colors that, when mixed in varying proportions, form all the other colors

prism a transparent body used to refract and spread out light

radio waves electromagnetic waves with a frequency below one billion hertz

real image an image that can be projected onto a surface

reflection the redirection or bouncing of light as it encounters a boundary between materials

refraction the bending of light as it passes from one material to another

resolution the ability to distinguish small objects

retina the thin set of cell layers at the back of the eye that process the image formed by the cornea and lens

scattering sending a beam of particles or rays into various directions

spectrum a set of frequencies

speed of light in a vacuum, visible light and other frequencies of electromagnetic radiation travel at 186,200 miles/second (300,000 km/s)

spontaneous   occurring naturally, with no external influence

terahertz   electromagnetic radiation with a frequency of about 1 to 30 trillion hertz

total internal reflection   complete reflection of light as it strikes a material with a lower index of refraction at a shallow angle

transparent   allowing light to pass through

ultraviolet   invisible electromagnetic radiation with a frequency slightly beyond that of violet light; the frequency range is roughly 750 trillion hertz to 2.4×10^{16} hertz

virtual image   an image produced by diverging rays that appear to be coming from a point; this kind of image cannot be projected on a surface

watt   a unit of power describing the amount of energy produced or consumed per second, equal to 0.00134 horsepower

wavelength   the distance of one full cycle of a wave

X-rays   electromagnetic radiation with a frequency between about 2.4×10^{16} and 5×10^{19} hertz

FURTHER READING AND WEB SITES

BOOKS

Bloomfield, Louis A. *How Things Work: The Physics of Everyday Life,* 3rd ed. New York: Wiley, 2005. This exceptional college-level text explains the physics behind a wide variety of everyday phenomena.

Bova, Ben. *The Story of Light.* Naperville, Ill.: Sourcebooks, 2001. Written by a prominent author of science books and science fiction novels, this book covers all the technological and scientific aspects of the subject.

Calle, Carlos I. *Superstrings and Other Things: A Guide to Physics.* Bristol: Institute of Physics, 2001. This book explains the laws and principles of physics in a clear and accessible manner.

Clegg, Brian. *Light Years and Time Travel: An Exploration of Mankind's Enduring Fascination with Light.* New York: Wiley, 2001. A fascinating chronicle of the history of attempts to understand the nature of light.

Harbison, James P. and Robert E. Nahory. *Lasers: Harnessing the Atom's Light.* New York: Scientific American Library, 1998. A readable and enjoyable introduction to the world of lasers.

Hecht, Jeff. *Optics: Light for a New Age.* New York: Charles Scribner's Sons, 1987. Written by an expert, this book introduces young adults to the science and technology of light.

Hubel, David H. *Eye, Brain, and Vision.* New York: Scientific American Library, 1988. An excellent and accessible book on the physiology of the visual system, written by one of the most noted vision researchers of the 20th century.

Kirkland, Kyle, and Sean M. Grady. *Optics: Illuminating the Power of Light.* New York: Facts On File, 2006. This book, intended for young adults, concentrates on the visible portion of the electromagnetic spectrum. It includes information on the history of optics, optical instruments and their construction, lasers, fiber optics, the visual system, and how the frontiers of optics are advancing scientific knowledge in biology, chemistry, astronomy, and physics.

Suplee, Curt. *The New Everyday Science Explained.* Washington D.C.: National Geographic Society, 2004. This richly illustrated book provides concise scientific answers to some of the most basic questions about people and nature.

WEB SITES

American Institute of Physics. "Physics Success Stories." Available online. URL: http://www.aip.org/success/. Accessed on August 11, 2006. Examples of how the study of physics has impacted society and technology.

American Physical Society. "Physics Central." Available online. URL: http://www.physicscentral.com/. Accessed on August 11, 2006. A collection of articles, illustrations, and photographs explaining physics and its applications, and introducing some of the physicists who are advancing the frontiers of physics even further.

Arecibo Observatory homepage. Available online. URL: http://www.naic.edu/. Accessed on August 11, 2006. News and information on one of the most prominent radio observatories in the world.

California Energy Commission. "The Energy Story: Chapter 15, Solar Energy." Available online. URL: http://www.energyquest.ca.gov/story/chapter15.html. Accessed on August 11, 2006. Part of a book describing the methods of producing energy and their impact on the world, this chapter discusses obtaining and transforming the energy in sunlight.

Exploratorium: The Museum of Science, Art and Human Perception. Available online. URL: http://www.exploratorium. edu/. Accessed on August 11, 2006. An excellent Web resource containing much information on the scientific explanations of everyday things.

Federal Communications Commission. "Wireless." Available online. URL: http://www.fcc.gov/cgb/cellular.html. Accessed on August 11, 2006. From the United States government agency charged with regulating communications, this Web page answers some of the frequency asked questions about cell phones. There are also links to other informative pages on wireless communication.

HowStuffWorks, Inc., homepage. Available online. URL: http:// www.howstuffworks.com/. Accessed on August 11, 2006. Contains a large number of articles, generally written by knowledgeable authors, explaining the science behind everything from computers to satellites.

Missile Defense Agency homepage. Available online. URL: http:// www.mda.mil. Accessed on August 11, 2006. News and information on missile defense, including the use of lasers to destroy missiles in flight.

National Aeronautics and Space Administration. Imagine the Universe. "Electromagnetic Spectrum." Available online. URL: http://imagine.gsfc.nasa.gov/docs/introduction/emspectrum. html. Accessed on August 11, 2006. A richly illustrated introduction to the spectrum of electromagnetic radiation.

———. "James Webb Space Telescope." Available online. URL: http://www.jwst.nasa.gov/. Accessed on August 11, 2006. Information on the development of the next generation space telescope.

———. "Space Optics." Available online. URL: http://optics.nasa. gov/index.html. Accessed on August 11, 2006. Descriptions of the various optical projects and technologies at NASA.

Nave, Carl R. "HyperPhysics Concepts." Available online. URL: http://hyperphysics.phy-astr.gsu.edu/hbase/hph.html. Accessed on August 11, 2006. This comprehensive resource for students offers illustrated explanations and examples of the basic concepts of all the branches of physics, including light and vision.

Space Telescope Science Institute. "Hubble Space Telescope." Available online. URL: http://hubblesite.org/. Accessed on August 11, 2006. This site contains information on the *Hubble Space Telescope,* along with plenty of breathtaking images of galaxies, nebulas, planets, and other astronomical bodies.

Vaccaro, Chris. "Understanding Weather Radar." Available online. URL: http://www.usatoday.com/weather/wearadar.htm. Accessed on August 11, 2006. This Web page explains how people gather weather information using radar.

Very Large Array (VLA) homepage. Available online. URL: http://www.vla.nrao.edu/. Accessed on August 11, 2006. News and information on the array of radio telescopes, located in New Mexico, which provide excellent resolution of radio sources in the sky.

Web Exhibits. "Colors: Why Things are Colored." Available online. URL: http://webexhibits.org/causesofcolor/index.html. Accessed on August 11, 2006. A thorough examination, with many examples, of the causes of color.

INDEX

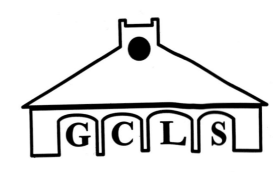

Gloucester County
Library System